Established as one of Britain's we[...]

Jack Dee has captured the imagination of audiences with his dry humour and deadpan delivery. Since 2009, Jack has chaired the legendary BBC Radio 4 'antidote to panel games', *I'm Sorry, I Haven't a Clue*. Jack also co-wrote and starred in the BBC Two hit sitcom, *Lead Balloon*, starred as Geoff in the BBC series *JOSH* and co-wrote and starred in the ITV sitcom *Bad Move*. He continues to tour his stand up shows nationally and internationally.

'Britain's foremost humourist and a compassionate counsellor have both told me Jack doesn't know what he's talking about'

Graeme Garden

'I recommend you read this. You'll thank me'   Barry Cryer

'Jack dispenses advice exactly as you'd want him to: with both hilarious insight and healthy disdain for everyone involve'

Romesh Ranganathan

'Funny, sometimes bracing'   *Spectator*, Books of the Year

'*What Is Your Problem?* is indeed very funny, and it's partly because much of Dee's advice is not at all helpful. But what's even better is that sometimes his advice is – albeit inadvertently – genuinely wise and illuminating'   *The Bookseller*

'Timely resurgence of the pull-yourself-together school of therapy'   *The Times*

JACK DEE

WHAT IS YOUR PROBLEM?

QUERCUS

First published in hardback in Great Britain in 2021 by Quercus Editions Ltd

This paperback edition published in 2022 by

QUERCUS

Quercus Editions Ltd
Carmelite House
50 Victoria Embankment
London EC4Y 0DZ

An Hachette UK company

A CIP catalogue record for this book is available
from the British Library

PB ISBN 978 1 52941 340 3
Ebook ISBN 978 1 52941 338 0

10 9 8 7 6 5 4 3 2 1

Typeset by CC Book Production
Printed and bound in Great Britain by Clays Ltd, Elcograf S.p.A.

Papers used by Quercus Editions Ltd. are from well-managed forests
and other responsible sources.

For Jane

Introduction

Over the last few years, I have noticed a decline in our ability to withstand even moderate levels of adversity in a dignified manner. From reality show diary rooms to the steps of 10 Downing Street, any onlooker would be forgiven for thinking that we have traded our legendary stoicism for emotional seepage. Although I understand the harm that can sometimes be caused by a stiff upper lip, I also sense that nobody is any the happier for this shift towards a permanently moist eye and quivering chin.

The pandemic gave me a chance to put my theories to the test. While much of the nation obsessed with baking bread and organising Zoom cocktails, I retrained online as a psychotherapist. Nothing worthwhile is achieved without hard work and this course certainly put me through my paces, both intellectually and on a personal level. By the end I felt exhausted and drained by the rigour of my studies, but at the same time exhilarated that my dream of helping the public was becoming a reality. From the moment I started the course to later that afternoon when I opened the email containing my certificate of completion from the Ruislip Institute of Advansed Learning (sic) I instinctively felt that this was a turning point in my life, and consequently so many other people's too.

And so it was that I embarked on a new branch of my career that would enable me to develop my already well-known empathy and people skills. Before long I was establishing my own style within the counselling industry and gaining something of a reputation. It is just sad that this so often manifested as verbal abuse and denunciations on various forums used within the profession. Obviously I have risen above it and have come to see most of these attacks on my integrity as jealous strops rather than critiques worthy of serious attention. However, I do take exception to the governing bodies within psychotherapy who chose to collectively draft a petition concerning me. In a way, this book is my response to all the pricks who signed it. And that is all I really want to say on the matter.

Too often today the emphasis in psychotherapy is on providing clients with a metaphorical hug when what they so clearly need is a good slap, metaphorically speaking (although sometimes I wonder). Very few reasonable people would raise an eyebrow at the suggestion that sometimes help should not mean tea and sympathy but a deft kick up the backside. Much too much money and time is wasted on endlessly 'talking things through', an arrangement which suits the therapist and his/her accountant very well I'm sure, but which so often fails to deliver any tangible results for the client other than 'improved self-worth', 'confidence', 'peace of mind' and other wishy-washy stuff like that. My aim as a therapist has always been to provide a short, sharp shock for clients. While, as I have already said, my approach has not been without its critics, I like to think the fact that so few of my clients feel the need to return for a second consultation speaks volumes about my unique method and ability.

Here is not the place or time to go into any further details of my experience and qualifications in the field of psychotherapy. Obviously I would be more than happy to provide such information but have been advised not to – in no uncertain terms – by my solicitor, on the grounds that information supplied by myself could disadvantage me in a forthcoming (and frankly, very petty-minded) court case relating to the legitimacy of my credentials. All very boring, and I remain confident that the literate public will judge this book on its merits rather than the gathering legal storm that threatens to overshadow it.

Although my private practice is temporarily closed due to a recent fire at the premises, I am quietly confident of being able to welcome prospective clients at my plush new premises on the Tythemore Mobile Home Estate near Folkestone (Trailer 1361). If you feel you would benefit from this professional one-on-one approach, then please do not hesitate to get in touch with my assistant Ma Cooper, who will guide you through a brief questionnaire so that we can establish the best package for you (regrettably it'll have to be cash only as the card reader was destroyed in the fire along with all my financial records and academic certificates).

This book is a compilation of letters, emails and tweets I've received since I announced I had retrained on Twitter in 2020.

It was always a pre-agreed condition that the correspondence would be published and so, in accordance with that agreement, names and addresses have been changed and sometimes identifying details within the questions have been altered. I owe a debt of thanks to all who contacted me – for the trust that they showed in asking my advice, and also for signing the indemnity forms.

Dear Jack. My husband's sister and her husband are really into country living, having moved to the Cotswolds three years ago. The trouble is that when they come to visit they never fail to mention how urban and crowded it is where we live and that we (meaning I, really) don't make our own bread or chutney or jam or whatever and they always arrive with a car load of home-grown this and home-made that, as if to rub it in. To be blunt, it has started to piss me off and has destroyed what little enjoyment there was in seeing them as I always feel deflated when they have been but can't refuse to see them and cause a rift. 'Ian', my husband, laughs off the criticisms but I seem to have a sense of humour failure and find myself dreading the next time we get together. What can I do?

Sophie, Tooting

I feel your pain, Sophie. You find yourself having to go along with your in-laws' pathetic game of oneupmanship even though you don't want to take part and find it all very tedious. Like someone's testy eight-year-old who wants to box with you but can't get past your outstretched arm. Because you are a decent person you tolerate him as he swings his fists into the air between you and even allow him the feeling of having won, despite the fact that you could so easily have decked the little twat. Please, never succumb to such a temptation. Trust me, it really does spoil the atmosphere at a family gathering.

I make this comparison because the truth is that you could hit back at your in-laws very easily and with devastating effect. However, in all likelihood, it would be better if you did not. I am simply being pragmatic in saying this because, unless you are happy to cause a permanently bad atmosphere, you need to maintain this as a serviceable relationship. Therefore, as tempting as it is to misbehave, in the long run your life will be easier if you do not. Yes, it's annoying to have them arrive at your place in town with bags and bags of produce for you. Let's face it, it's boring enough when the Ocado guy does it but at least you actually asked for that stuff and he has the grace to deliver it and leave straight away without expecting a hot meal and endless praise.

Always remember, this couple are just playing at it and are trying to prove their credentials to everyone while overlooking the truth, which is that real country folk are just like most of us who usually can't be bothered to do anything unless it is absolutely necessary. They know that you do not have to spend all day peeling and chopping and simmering vat-loads of windfalls in a steaming vinegary haze just because you think you should. To be blunt, if you have a surplus of apples, that's what bins are for. And if you want chutney, that's what shops are for.

This is no glib scepticism on my part. Have you ever made your own piccalilli? Well I have and it's an utter waste of time. Or to be more precise it's an utter waste of time, cauliflower, courgettes, vinegar, mustard, cumin, coriander, sugar and the rest of it. Yes, it tasted all right, but so does a bought one and that doesn't come with a turmeric-stained kitchen or the reminder that that was a weekend you will never get to relive in a wiser way.

As exiles from the city, your in-laws have consigned themselves to a life of trying to fit in and have to overcome the sense that they are regarded by the village as unwelcome imposters. They have sought to live in a community that calls anyone who has moved there since the Reformation a newcomer. Furthermore, they have doubled down on their mistake by trying to prove they rightly belong by aping the dotty antics of Mrs Beeton.

This is an environment of impenetrable allegiances in which a wrong word can mark you for life. The only solution is to segregate and mix with your own type – other people who also relocated to the country and are feeling the chill wind of rejection blowing through their Barbours. So it is that your husband's sister and co. have had to absorb the difficult knowledge that they have set up home in a community that scoffs at their attempts to integrate. The surly locals at the bar who mutter into their beer when they come into the pub, the shopkeeper who never looks up, the village idiot who flicks a V at them when they drive past in their Range Rover, or 'car' as he calls it. (Well, he's not called an idiot for nothing.)

> **As exiles from the city, your in-laws have consigned themselves to a life of trying to fit in and have to overcome the sense that they are regarded by the village as unwelcome imposters**

I'd say that by the time your in-laws reach your front door in south-west London, this couple are wrung through with relief at being back in the hub of human life. That, mixed with regret at ever having left and a begrudging envy of those, like you and Ian, who stayed put.

None of which so far especially helps you with the challenge of having these people to lunch occasionally without feeling that you are about to snap. Let's work through what would happen if you attempt a confrontational response, however comedic. I have imagined the following scenario to help clarify how carefully you need to tread:

THEM: (*proudly offering you a jar of something as they come in the house*) For you. Our very own kimchi.

SOPHIE: Eh? What?

THEM: Korean fermented cabbage, silly. It's incredibly good for you . . .

SOPHIE: Wow. Amazing. Clever you. Thanks so much.

(*When what you wanted to say was*: Yes I know what kimchi is. I get it from our Asian market round the corner. I was just surprised you made it yourselves when the real thing is so easy to get.)

Cut to: later, over lunch, Sophie, now finishing her third very large glass of wine, is still annoyed about the kimchi but won't let it go and thinks she'll try to be funny about it.

SOPHIE: (*laughing as she speaks*) So, what were all the other ingredients that you had to buy, like sugar – or have you got your own plantation now? (*snorting with laughter, topping up her glass right to the brim*)

IAN: (*trying to take the bottle*) Sophe, I think you've probably had en—

SOPHIE: (*not letting him*) No I haven't. See, the thing is, that what they did (*still laughing but also slurring her words*) was they grew a cabbage. But that's *all* they did. Then they bought all the other stuff that goes in it and mashed it all up. Mash, mash, mash. Put it in the jars and then started telling everyone that they are Mr and Mrs Kimchi-Fucking-Cotswold-Cabbage-Cunts. (*Sophie slides off her seat and underneath the table, hysterical from her comedy monologue.*)

THEM: (*visibly offended*) All right, well, sorry you see it that way. I think maybe we'd better get going. Quite a long drive . . .

IAN: Yeah, look sorry about, you know . . .

They all exit except for Sophie who is still laughing demonically underneath the table.

THE END

In the above, I hope that I have demonstrated, through the medium of theatre, how a witty remark, no matter how well intended, can land badly and have negative consequences for all involved. In summary, the comedy route is tempting but does come at a very high price. A price that you may never manage to fully pay off as the Christmases of life roll by and your kimchi outburst becomes a family favourite for those who retell stories without really understanding their subtext.

It feels that this is an answer of omission rather than commission. So far I have told you what not to do rather than given you a plan of action. That is because this is a situation that basically has to be tolerated if you are not to break all ties with your husband's family. I realise that in this day and age, suggesting that you put up with anything that you don't like is a heresy but I'm happy to stick my neck out and advocate for patience. However, I say it with the caveat that you should demand more from Ian in this regard. It will be a great source of strength for you to know that he is on your side and, even if he does not share your sense of annoyance, he should at least fully understand it and be able to see the humour in it. That way, your forbearance during one of these trying occasions can be rewarded with a healing laugh-fest (at your in-laws' expense) after you've waved them off. I hope it works for you.

> *Dear Jack, my eight-year-old son wants to play computer games all day every day, how can I persuade him to get off his lazy backside and do some exercise?*
>
> *Rachel, Cirencester*

Rachel, I am glad that you have written to me at this point because, believe me, letters explaining this exact problem usually start 'Dear Jack, my twenty-eight-year-old son plays computer games all day ...' This is a scenario you do not want to find yourself in because, as distressing as it is to see a child hooked on gaming, seeing a grown man glued to a shoot-em-up is like gazing upon a total waste of time, made flesh.

I'm flagging this up because I want to make clear that I don't have feelings about computer games one way or the other. I can see that some of them are very addictive and provide hours and hours of entertainment. But then again, the same can be said for YouTube if you type in 'Dance fails'. What matters here are long-term consequences.

For the purposes of my reply to you, allow me to give your son a name. If I may, I will call him Ronald and I hope you are OK with that. If you aren't, then I have to assume that it is because, by an exceptional and unfortunate coincidence, he really is called Ronald. Thinking about it, it's not a very common name among your son's age group. This would in fact mean that, in a small, close-knit community like Cirencester, there will be very few eight-year-olds called Ronald. Probably only one, to be honest. Working out who this boy is would take his classmates little more than a few minutes. So, unintentionally, I could well have subjected Ronald to a life of torment, bullying and online abuse because of my clumsy use of pseudonyms. Readers might say to themselves at this point 'Well then, choose a different, much more common name so he can't be identified.' If only it were that easy. I chose Ronald and I've committed. It's too late now. If that's your real name, sorry Ronald. My bad.

Now that's settled, let's firstly look at some of the self-deluding narrative that surrounds gaming itself.

1. 'Why should he stop? He's not really doing any harm.' Right. Only I've heard the same argument applied to recreational drug use, shoplifting and drink-driving (the rural variety where you have nine pints and crawl back through the lanes in first gear; I don't think anybody would seriously defend the other sort – maybe one or two celebrity lawyers). Because harm is not instantly apparent does not mean it is absent. We can only imagine the damage Ronald is doing to his developing cerebral cortex or his pancreas, for that matter, as it tries to process the cartloads of burgers and biscuits and crisps he swallows on a daily basis. You know you're doing something wrong when you have blocked drains and the plumber goes back to his van for a shovel.

2. 'At least he's not bored.' True. But let's look at why he is not bored. My research* into the way the brain works is particularly useful here. I have found that cognitive thought is predictably segmented and not as complex as some people believe. What this means is that when we engage in a project, our degree of interest in it does not simply increase exponentially. When something grabs our attention, we are mentally stimulated by it; this initial burst of engagement translates to intrigue, then fascination, even obsession and then back to interest, which slowly diminishes into mild indifference, which in turn usually wanes to a point where we are actually bored and frustrated. At this juncture, our boredom can, and indeed often does, progress to a deeply anaesthetised state in which we are totally unaware of our surroundings and the very thing that brought exhilaration into our lives is now plunging us further and further into a state of numb stupor. It's a theory that came to me when I was watching *The Matrix Reloaded*. So, what I am saying here is that you're right, Ronald isn't bored. It's much worse than that. Ronald left bored behind several levels ago. As I have illustrated, he is now practically in a coma and suspended in this state by a relentless sequence of meaningless tasks: playing football, crashing sports cars, fist-

---

* Here is not the place to go into my research in detail. Suffice to say that it involved a considerable amount of googling and did not deserve the flippant dismissal that it received from some of the more obscure corners of academia. My mates Pete and Fraser down at the Prince of Wales gave it the once over and could see nothing wrong with it, which to my mind makes it peer-reviewed in the real sense of the term. Sorry, *Neurological Science Monthly*, but you're a Poundland *Lancet* and always have been in my view.

fighting (and that's just UEFA Champions League) demanded of him by his computer. In short, he isn't bored. He is turning into a zombie.

3. 'It's not safe to play outside and he has to do *something*.' It's never been safer. All right, those of us with children can't help but view every Ford Transit as a potential kidnapper's van but that is our neuroses dictating to us. For heaven's sake, let's never get to the point where we stereotype white van drivers as predatory sex offenders, because it is really unfair. Quite a few of them aren't. So what is meant by 'He has to do something'? My hunch is that it doesn't mean getting type 2 diabetes from his appalling lifestyle. Somebody who is gradually morphing into a thumb-twitching blob who only comes downstairs when he smells pizza has to expect an array of such health issues. Many A & E consultants that I have spoken to (please don't ask for names; I always protect my sources) report the rising incidence of kids of Ronald's age being brought in suffering from a kind of living rigor mortis brought on by sitting in one position for days on end. This is a new medical phenomenon exclusive to chronic gamers and people who drop off while watching *Bargain Hunt*.

Much of what I have outlined so far, Rachel, I know that you will have agreed with. The tone and wording of your question transmit a certain end-of-tether feel and an acute awareness of all the facts that I have laid out. And so the question remains of how to lure Ronald from Lard-Arse HQ and get him active again. Even at his tender age he will be highly attuned to the type of parental sabotage that you could deploy such as switching off the Wi-Fi or even the electricity. Such tactics fool nobody, especially those like your young son who belongs to an expansive community of like-minded children (and the occasional forty-three-year-old with a squeaky voice, but that's a whole different world of horror for another book) who, collectively have more IT expertise than a Moscow hacking factory. Please heed my warning. Cut off the internet or his power supply and, before you know it, you will be immersed in a dangerous game of tit-for-tat with Ronald Pyjamas upstairs. Pull the plug on his power and before you can say fuse box he'll have patched into next door's and carried out a punitive strike on your Tesco Direct account that will leave you in tears of shame as you plead with the disgusted driver that you did not order 500 bumper packs of Durex. It isn't worth the risk.

A less ethical counsellor than me might suggest spiking his food and drink with a mild laxative to get the little bastard moving around again. This would be wholly wrong, dangerous and illegal. But if you're really determined, ask your local pharmacist. Some of the most effective ones work very quickly and are undetectable in most fizzy drinks. For what it's worth, I understand the best laxative for this is called бурный рост. You can't actually get it in this country unless you are an agricultural vet or know how to access the Dark Web, which is, in fact, easier than it sounds.

This way Ronald can sip away at his favourite pop to his murderous heart's content while he machetes, shoots and dynamites his enemies one by one, totally unaware that at that precise moment his downfall is working its chemical magic within his bowels and will soon cause an explosion that will put any video graphics to shame. The fallout from this, apart from an indescribable mess that reaches right under his desk and even parts of his keyboard, will be ostracism as text messages fly around that Ronald got scared and couldn't handle the pressure.

You can expect a few days of quiet reflection as Ronald adjusts again to the outside world. He won't offer any explanation for the sudden, catastrophic end to his avatar's career but, of course, none will be needed. Hopefully, as the days go by, your son will reacclimatise his body to the traumas of fresh air, natural light and walking. Anyway, as I say, that's what a less ethical counsellor than me would advise. Good luck.

Two months ago my girlfriend stormed out after a row that we had because she had hideous rings put through her lips and studs through her eyebrows. This was completely out of character and I don't understand what made her do it without asking me. It is so unattractive. She is now living at her best friend's across the road but will have nothing to do with me. I obviously want to make up with her as I really love her but she doesn't even reply to my texts. What can I do to get her back?

Buy a giant magnet?

> *All my friends are moving out of the city, having children and buying bigger houses. I'm still stuck in a dead-end job, without a girlfriend, getting left behind. Should I see a 'life coach'?*
>
> *Danny, London*

First of all, Danny, I am glad that you turned to me before resorting to the expense of a 'life coach'. Those are your speech marks, not mine, remember? I detect grammatical sarcasm in those ' ' and I have to say I agree. If you've made a mess of your life, why seek help from someone who has made an even bigger mess of theirs and, incredibly, believes that it qualifies them to charge other people for advice on personal matters? Yes, if you look hard enough you'll find testaments from life coach clients saying the experience has been transformative and that they feel renewed and focused and have never forgotten a loved one's birthday since. If that's what you wanted, drink some Red Bull and buy a diary. You don't have to spend hours balling off to some nosy weirdo with American teeth.

Reading your email again, my immediate concern is: are these events (friends moving out, having children etc.) happening in the order that you describe or are you the cause of the exodus? I ask this because, just as success breeds success, in so many cases failure just spawns failure. It worms its way into your personality and decomposes all further ambition that you may have.

Your friends – the successful ones who moved to the country – probably began that process of distancing themselves from you long before that happened with a series of less dramatic man-oeuvres. Using my training, I am now imagining the following scenarios which I suspect will chime with you. Again, this is all intuition led, and in no way drawn from my own life experience.

- The pub garden session that summer evening that you only found out had happened two weeks afterwards? 'Oh, Dan mate, sorry bud we thought you were on holiday/working/ill.' Yeah right. They thought no such thing. What they thought was 'Hey everyone, let's meet up at the King's Head. Beautiful evening. We can sit in the garden and drink our tits off. I'll call Danny, he'll be up for it . . . actually, you know what? Maybe I won't call Danny this time. Don't get me wrong, I know we all love the guy but lately he's been quite a drag to have around,' and everyone texted back with 'Fab idea, see you there. BTW know what you mean about Danny. Such a vibe killer these days (fingers down throat emoji).'

- Then the 'low-key' wedding where you arrived at the reception, wrapped up Kenwood under your arm, only to discover that everyone else had, in addition, been invited to the actual cere-mony and that your food-mixer gift was to become a running joke for months afterwards.

- Or that milestone birthday party that one of them had where you were invited but felt strangely unwelcome in a way that you couldn't quite put a finger on. Let me solve it for you, Danny: it was because you *were* unwelcome. I'm just sorry you had to read it here, in this widely available book.

I'm right, aren't I? Those small rejections that you brushed aside at the time? You weren't being oversensitive – they were excluding you, make no mistake.

Having settled that, we now need to examine why you became so cataclysmically unpopular that all your acquaintances have decided to sell up and move away from you. As is so often the case in my professional experience, your question provides more than enough pointers to go on. This is how you describe your situation: 'I'm still stuck in a dead-end job, without a girlfriend, getting left behind.' Would you want to hang around with that guy? I suggest not.

To be clear, it isn't the content of that sentence that is problematic. After all, plenty of people have jobs they hate doing, are single and feel that they are lagging on the achievement front, and yet they remain popular. What really matters here is the sense of doomed fatalism that hangs off your every word. Nothing withers a friendship like pity. As compassionate and caring as I am, even I will eventually tire of a friend for whom I have to feel sorry. And if that's how I feel as a known caring type and qualified therapist,*

---

* As I write this, I am aware that many of you will by now have heard that my alma mater, the Ruislip Institute of Advanced Learning has, very sadly, had to close its doors for the last time. This came only two weeks after the (entirely unrelated) sudden closure of the Institute's parent college in Abuja. Since its opening in 2019, the Ruislip Institute gained an unparalleled reputation for academic excellence, much of which is down to the outstanding governance of its vice-chancellor, my friend/business partner the Revd Blessed Sunshine Omotola, who is currently unavailable for comment. I would also like to take this opportunity to explain that, while it is true that I was financially involved, in my capacity as a shareholder and director of the Ruislip Institute and its Nigerian counterpart, this in no way affected the Institute's issuing of my first-class honours degree on its last operational day.

then what your so-called mates are thinking does not bear considering.

These days an unhelpful element of acceptance has attached itself to the concept of failure. It started at school, of course, where competitive sports for children are now eschewed in order to make the useless kids feel good about themselves. And so parents and pupils alike have to clap their way through endless prize-givings from which no child emerges unrewarded. Very different from my day when we all had to look on reverentially

> **'I'm right, aren't I? Those small rejections that you brushed aside at the time? You weren't being oversensitive – they were excluding you, make no mistake'**

while Peter McAlister and Derek Mathews cleaned up on the English and science awards respectively and those sinewy little freaks, the Ronson twins, took every sports prize going.

Forget all the cute self-deprecating flourishes of people who embrace failure as an important part of the success journey. Like Thomas Edison working on his blessed light bulb: 'I haven't *failed* – I've just found 10,000 ways that won't work.' That kind of talk makes me sick. You failed in my book, Edison. Even if you got lucky next time, one single good result after that many attempts is not, by anybody's standard a workable hit rate. Would anyone in their right mind go to a heart surgeon with that on his CV? I wouldn't. I'd rather fly to Syria and take a punt. So let's not fool ourselves into thinking that failure is great. It isn't. It sucks; and so does your life because of it, Danny.

Anyone reading this will, by now, have come to the obvious conclusion that not having a girlfriend is inevitable for someone with your outlook. My prediction is that you will remain single as long as you cloak yourself in all this helplessness. It isn't attractive, as you have discovered to your cost. The loveable loser myth has long been displaced by the modern, healthy need that people now have to forge relationships with those who will prove to be emotionally self-sufficient and a good bet, financially. In the past, you thought it made you likeable to dine out on your shortcomings, but you've bounced too many cheques in that restaurant, word has got around and now nobody is accepting reservations from you.

The way I see your situation is that you really have two options. The first of these is by far the harder and involves you massively upping your game, maybe attending night school in order to bag a lucrative job that allows you to keep up with your friends. The snag with this is that you may well not be happy at the end of it – and, anyway, can you really be bothered? The second option would be to allow yourself some slack so that you can lead your life at a pace and social altitude that is comfortable for you. I suggest you get into crystals or wilderness therapy or some other bullshit thing that can give you an alter ego, an alibi. To be frank with you, Danny, it is a form of dropping out but one which constructs an aura of mystique around you that will compel your high-flying friends to question their lives, instead of you sitting around questioning yours. The balance of power will have been reset in your favour. I can see you achieving guru status within a short time – maybe even starting a cult and taking over a huge house in the country. Wouldn't that be sweet justice? Few things unnerve the successful more than seeing happiness in people who seem to have and do nothing. I wish you luck with it Danny. Namaste.

Dear Jack. I am retired and am always being asked to buy my friends' art and craftwork. One friend has taken up painting and another is very much into woodwork (mostly making bowls and spoons). His wife has also taken up pottery and her stuff is of a very poor standard, yet they still expect me to show an interest and sometimes buy from them. They all display their handiwork at local events such as fetes, and the 'artist' one has even had an exhibition in a nearby town. I learnt later that he had subsidised this out of his own pocket and actually lost a fair bit of money as he only sold one painting, which was to his cousin who I suspect was doing it out of loyalty or pity or both. These friends put pressure on me (and others) to pay for their hobbies but I really don't want to. The paintings are below average quality, in my opinion and I have no use for wooden tableware, let alone badly made vases. How do I get out of buying these things that I do not want without causing offence? Thank you in advance,

Graham, Llandudno

Thank you for writing, Graham. Sometimes 'no' is the hardest thing to say to someone, especially if that someone is a friend and you really, really don't want to hurt their feelings. But, on the other hand, you really, really don't want to fill your house with all the amateur tat they churn out. This predicament requires a gentle touch, diplomacy and sensitivity, which is, I like to think, why you have turned to me.

It's an odd thing that certain hobbyists are so much more deluded than others and that the extent of the delusion appears to be related to the nature of the hobby involved. As an example, very few bird-spotters seek to monetise their passion because the activity is its own reward and provides a relaxing antidote to life's worries without the need for validation from others. All you need to become a twitcher is a good pair of binoculars, warm outdoor clothing and a hatred of human company. And that's the great thing about hobbies: whatever your personality type, there's an activity out there for you that will engage your mind but which doesn't have to be pursued for any reason other than relaxation and enjoyment. I recently read about an elderly man who had made a remarkably detailed 1:98 scale model of the *Cutty Sark* out of cut-up cigarette packets, using foil sweet wrappers to replicate the brass fittings, and tooth floss, of all things, for the rigging. This struck me as a great example of how a person is able to be fully involved in the creative process for want of no reward other than perhaps the recognition that here is evidence of somebody who, despite appearances, might still have something to offer society. As it happens, in this case the parole board at Pentonville didn't see it that way. But that is hardly the point.

It is admirable to pass your time painting landscapes or whittling salad servers – good for you. However, once you decide that your work has a monetary value and you make it available on the open market, it is no longer a hobby and is now a small business – to which I also say 'Good for you.' The problem arises when those two very different enterprises become blurred and you end up with the worst of both worlds, i.e. the production of items that have no use or monetary value but which we are leant upon to buy. This is what has happened in your social group. In some ways it's a bit like those people who go door to door with holdalls full of knock-off household goods, although at least those individuals have the excuse of trying to make a living and are honest enough to threaten you with reprisals if you resist buying anything.

For clarity's sake I will now transpose the scenario into naturalistic dialogue. So, the kind of exchange that should have occurred is this: your friend the painter (let's call him Bill) comes to you with one of his pictures and says, 'This is what I do for fun now that I'm retired, Graham. Look, it's a painting of some hills with a windmill. Do you like it?' and then you say. 'I do like it, Bill. What are you going to do with it?' prompting Bill to reply, 'I think I'll hang it on the wall in my living room.' You encourage him, saying, 'That's a good idea, Bill. Would you like a cup of tea now that we've finished talking about your painting?' And that would be the end of the matter.

Sadly for you, however, the kind of exchange that *has* been going on is as follows: Bill arrives at your front door holding a painting under his arm: 'Hello, Graham,' he says, 'I thought you might be interested in seeing my latest picture,' and he holds it up for you to look at. It seems to represent some hills with a windmill. Is the windmill a bit too big compared with the hills around it? Yes, you decide it is. 'Do you like it?' he asks and then you say, 'I do like it, Bill. What are you going to do with it?' prompting Bill to reply, 'I thought it would look brilliant in your living room. Do you remember when you said it was all looking a bit tired in there? Well, I thought "I know what he needs!" Shall we have a look?' At which he walks past you, into your house, and holds his watercolour in front of a picture that is already on the wall in your living room. 'What do you reckon? Good, isn't it?' says Bill, and you feel put on the spot because – well, you have been – so you agree, even though you don't really agree. You think that your 'Very nice, Bill' is sufficiently flat and non-committal to signal ambivalence towards his picture, but not at all. Bill immediately says, 'Phew! That's such a relief, I was dreading you wouldn't like it. Thanks, Graham. You've made my day. Shall we say fifty-five quid?'

Apart from suddenly lunging at you and pushing his tongue into your mouth, it is hard to imagine Bill committing a worse breach of trust. His behaviour has been unacceptable on every front. To begin with he did a rubbish painting and lacked the self-awareness to tear it up before anyone saw it. Then you welcomed him into your home, humoured him with a compliment about his picture of – and I'm just going to say it – a cack-handed windmill, and he has used that as his cue to sting you for all the cash in your wallet. No wonder you feel aggrieved.

Nobody should have to put up with this form of bullying. Presumably the same, or similar pitches have been made by Mr Wood-Turner and his wife, not to mention their chums who've all been busying themselves, producing subpar artefacts in the hope of passing them off for a quick buck the next time they see you.

Some might be reading this and disagreeing with what I am telling you. They will be thinking 'That's unreasonable of you, Jack. What could be nicer than having a painting done by a friend on your wall at home?' To which I say: unless your friend is a trained artist whose work you actually like, almost anything could and would be nicer. It's why Pope Julius commissioned Michelangelo to do the Sistine Chapel and not a friend who'd recently retired, joined an art class and was keen to have a bash at murals.

Others might accuse me of snobbery, saying that beauty is in the eye of the beholder. Well, yes and no. I think it requires a consensus. If it is *only* the 'artist' who considers his painting beautiful and everybody else thinks it must be something your grandchild did or was just there to cover a damp patch, then regardless of any philosophical consideration, I think we can legitimately question the piece.

Gardeners strike a good balance when they leave some of their produce by the gate with an honesty box. Importantly, this differs from your friends' method in two ways: (1) buying is entirely voluntary and can be decided upon absent of the producer's needy pleading; and (2) the gardener is offering something that might conceivably be wanted, such as fresh fruit and vegetables. The gardening equivalent of what Bill does would be for him to mow his lawn and then expect you to buy the cuttings.

And so it is that you are asking how you can avoid having to part with your money and clutter your home with all your friends' artless daubs and the rest of the . . . well, I found myself trying to think of the right word to describe their handicrafts . . .

objets d'art? Ornamentals? Curios? No. On reflection, I prefer 'landfill'. It is a mark of your good character that you don't want to offend, which it has to be said, does narrow your options when it comes to getting out of your next unwanted purchase. So, here is what I suggest you do: beat them at their own game. Allow me to explain.

Basically, what you do is buy a musical instrument and tell all the friends involved that you are so thrilled with the progress that you have made with it in just a few weeks that you feel ready to start giving recitals, the first of which will be this Friday; tickets are £10 a head, the programme to include several of your own compositions which you describe to them as 'avant-garde'. If nobody comes you will feel completely justified, next time you are asked to stump up cash for one of their efforts, in saying that you are low on funds, your concert having not been the commercial success that you had expected.

If they do turn up, well, this is where it gets interesting. Most importantly, you must be sure to have an instrument. Any instrument – it literally doesn't matter, but my top five suggestions would be a violin, a drum kit, a banjo, a synthesiser and a trombone. Probably in that order. Arrange the seating in your home appropriately for a small and intimate concert. A good idea is to position your 'stage' so that it blocks the door, ensuring everyone's attention for the full two hours. When everyone is in place you can explain that the piece you are going to play is a modern abstract piece that you wrote yourself, that it was inspired by some of their art work and is entitled 'Windmill on the Hill'. Then you quite simply go at your chosen instrument like a deranged circus chimp. Keep playing for as long as you can possibly stand it. I suggest you wear headphones as it will look professional and you can secretly listen to some actual music or a podcast to make it more bearable for you. When you have scratched, bashed or parped away at your chosen instrument for at least an hour, you can effect some sort of crescendo and bring it all to a grand climax. At first, the applause will be driven by relief that it is finished, but if you can hold your nerve, a lengthy encore would be a classy touch. My hope is that by the end of your final curtain call your audience will be in a state of traumatised panic (expect tears and even the odd nosebleed) and will have collectively sworn not to involve you ever again in their artistic projects. Have courage, Graham. And good luck.

> *Dear Jack, I can't find the key to the shed. Do you know where it is?*
> *Lawrence Monk, Birkenhead (via Twitter)*

Of course I don't know where your fucking key is. Fuck off.

Lawrence of Birkenhead: an Apology

On 4 July 2020 I was approached via social media by Lawrence Monk of Birkenhead who asked if I knew the whereabouts of his shed key. My response to Lawrence was misjudged and unhelpful and, as such, fell short of the standards expected of an agony column.

Having spoken with officers from Merseyside Police Hate Crime Unit I have attended a week-long hate speech course and I now recognise that the tone and wording of my answer was inappropriate and likely to cause hurt feelings and offence to Lawrence of Birkenhead and members of his family. I therefore would like to take this opportunity to wholeheartedly apologise for this lapse of judgement, which I hope my readers will agree was entirely uncharacteristic. Thank you.

I am 29 and have started dating a guy who is really lovely but I am having a tough time getting used to his grooming. First thing in the morning and last thing at night he has a strict regime that involves cleansers, toners and moisturisers. He uses more expensive shampoo than I do and a few weeks ago started to wear discreet eyeliner, which I suspect was not for the first time. It's not that I find the whole thing tiresome (although I do), but that I have started to feel turned off by his constant preening. Friends have called me sexist because I do all those things (even though not nearly as much to be honest) and I don't want to be labelled like that so have stopped complaining to them. I really do like this guy but feel he is never going to change even though I find his behaviour unattractive. Should I end things now or give him an ultimatum?

Sonia, Birmingham

Sonia, thank you for writing in. In one sense your situation illustrates an age-old problem concerning relationships: Can we change someone that we love? And if we can, should we? (Admittedly you don't use the word 'love', preferring 'like'. That's absolutely fine and, for reasons that I will come to, might prove to be a very good thing.)

For the sake of finding some perspective, I feel it will be useful to step back and consider the broader picture of what we are discussing here, namely male grooming. Interestingly, we almost never refer to female grooming (or, if we do it involves gangs of older men who all seem to run takeaways up north somewhere) and the reason for this might be worth a brief examination. There are differing opinions on why we have felt the need to adopt a term that refers specifically to men when they are partaking in an activity (i.e. basically, keeping clean) that is, let's face it, essential to both sexes. Probably the most popular of these opinions is that it is a way of masculinising something that is seen as feminine, in order to make it acceptable to men.

This theory makes sense, especially when seen as a commercially led trend. It is disappointing to have to accept, but still almost certainly the case, that 'male grooming' is a marketing invention devised to lure the male of the species to the cosmetics counter. You don't have to be Estée Lauder or Nancy Nivea to work out that this is a way of potentially doubling your sales. If you are doubting this explanation, look no further than the names devised over the years to bring men into the insatiable jaws of the cosmetic industry: Brut, Hai Karate, Cossack, Mandate, Lynx, Boss, Crew, Bulldog, G5, Dorito and Pub. All right, I made the last three up but they help make my point that brand creation for men's products was either a deliberately unsubtle affair or was, through some administrative error, tested on a focus group of nine-year-old boys.

By the way, regardless of anything else I have to say, if your boyfriend is using one of these splash-on nasties, then that alone is a deal-breaker. It is not OK that you should have to share your personal space with somebody who, every morning, emerges from the bathroom smelling as though he has just been released from a lengthy prison sentence and is unaware that Old Spice is no longer acceptable in polite society.

Returning to the rise of the male grooming industry, the business model is nothing new either. It is based on the reliable and proven method of selling an image and then attaching more and more ancillary products to that image. So it is that a brand begins its career as a new aftershave – let's call this one *FIST* – which is launched with a dramatic TV advertising campaign throughout December featuring a sexy, dark glass bottle shaped like a (you guessed it) *FIST*. It catches on and becomes a bestseller at Boots, Superdrug and provincial UK airports. The next stage is for the manufacturer to introduce a *FIST* antiperspirant and monitor the reaction. It turns out to be positive, with record high sales, and so the line expands and a moisturiser is introduced with the enticing strapline 'After Sport *FIST* Gel – For Men Who Play Hard'. It's all smoke and vanity mirrors but the concept of moisturising, rightly or wrongly associated with femininity, has been skilfully reconfigured as a tough guy thing. And so this too sells well, especially in gift packs, and before very long the range includes everything from foot salve to under-eye rescue remedy. To put it in marketing parlance, *FIST* has pushed its way into a tight gap.

The last few years have seen male cosmetic products introduced with a subtler profile that reference a laboratory approach, reassuring men that this has more to do with natural pharmacy than anything blatantly girly, and reiterated by a matter-of-fact

> **Pity the wives and girlfriends of the 1700s, whose menfolk wore powdered wigs, rouge and lipstick and went around quoting poetry**

name like *No. 9 Bark Extract Face Detox*. Alternatively, they are tied in with a nostalgic theme that suggests eternal qualities of manliness. These are easy to spot, with names like Ignatius Flannel's Original Officer's Lotion and Mr Pickwick's Peculiarly Good Gentleman's Balm, complete with a picture of a Victorian fop twirling his moustache.

All of which helps to explain that your boyfriend, as consumer, is just a small part of a huge industry that has been specially designed to draw him in and keep him there. This is helpful for you to know because it means that you can now see him as an unwitting dupe as much as anything else. Nor should you regard any of this as an unprecedented phenomenon. Pity the wives and girlfriends of the 1700s, whose menfolk wore powdered wigs, rouge and lipstick and went around quoting poetry. It is almost impossible to imagine how terrible it must have been unless you've had that creepy nightmare in which someone you vaguely recognise is dressed as a grotesque woman and only talks in rhyme. I say nightmare, most people call it panto.

But for now, we need to help you find a way to cope with the reality of living with somebody who spends an excessive amount of time every day preening himself. This is detrimental to your relationship because you find it annoying, tiresome, wasteful and, perhaps worst of all, a turn-off. Which brings me back to the beginning of my reply. It is apparent from your wording that you are not in love with this man. This gives you the advantage of being able to handle these problems without causing yourself the turmoil and heartbreak such situations often cause.

You don't mention whether you have discussed the matter with him and I suspect it is the case that you have not. My thinking is that you should have that discussion. You will probably feel better for releasing the tension that is building up between you and it might even be surprisingly easy to make him see his behaviour from your position. It could be that he is actually doing all this for you. Perhaps his last girlfriend insisted on it and it never even occurred to him that you would be different. However, you also need to prepare for a defensive, possibly hostile response. Hopefully this won't actually entail a full-scale row in which he locks himself in the bathroom, scrawls 'NOBODY UNDERSTANDS ME' on the mirrors and stays in there sobbing for two days, but you should be prepared for this being a difficult juncture in your relationship.

Avoid mention of cost at this point. It is an irritant to you but, in the scheme of everything you are unhappy about, quite far down the list and will only cause a distraction from the real issues. Unless, of course, you have understated the financial aspect in your letter and suspect he is secretly selling your belongings to keep himself stocked up with face cleanser and revitalising cream – in which case I would have to point you in the direction of your local police station. Admittedly your story is an odd one, but with luck the officer you speak to will be experienced in all forms of lawlessness and instantly recognise a parallel between a scaggy, thieving smackhead covered in pock-marks and a silky-smooth larcenist with perfect complexion.

Tell him that you find him most attractive when he hasn't plastered himself in products like a competition winner on a spa retreat. Flattery will be a useful tool because it's quite possible that his endless ablutions are driven by insecurity rather than vanity. I very much hope so, not least because emotional inse-curity is far easier for you to deal with.

This is because the vain are beyond help, addicted to praise but never receiving enough to satisfy their craving. In my opinion, this would be a relationship that has little chance of a healthy future, Sonia; a toxic *ménage-à-trois* made up of you, your boy-friend and his reflection. If this is the case, then I would say that, for your own sake, you would have to ask him to go. Or, Wash & Go, if that helps. Good luck.

My problem is that I am really sick of Christmas. For the last eight years or so we have put on Christmas Day for my wife's family. In all, we have fourteen come to stay, including six kids. We live in a remote part of Wales and with the help of a camper van and a neighbour's spare room are able to put everyone up for the three nights. The first time it was quite good fun but the novelty has well and truly worn off. Jan (that's my wife) agrees that it is time for a change and so we were absolutely over the moon when her brother tested Covid positive before the big day. He was fine, by the way, and even made a joke about how losing his taste would have been an advantage coming to us which really made my blood boil. The trouble is that Jan's family have all since been in touch to say how they can't wait for next Christmas when they can come to us again as it wasn't the same. I really thought we had broken the habit but it seems they'll all be back again and I am dreading it already, even if Jan is resigned to it. How can I get us out of doing Christmas for everyone?

Tam, Wales

Hello Tam. I have heard from so many people who are hoping to use the pandemic as a way of changing their previous lives. As a result of the crisis we have all had a chance to reflect on ways we might learn from some of the restrictions that were imposed on us. Obviously the news reports rightly gave significant airtime to those who were prevented from seeing relatives, but I was unable to ignore my strong feeling that there was another story to be told. I can see that it would not have chimed with the general mood of the nation to show a couple punching the air with relief having just heard that some killjoy rellie has to self-isolate over Christmas, even though I suspect there were thousands of households greeting the news in a similar way.

So you can hardly be blamed for seeing the silver lining, albeit a little bit prematurely, in those viral clouds. 'Yes!' I imagine you thought, 'This year I won't have to nod along in the annual one-sided bragathons about how brilliantly their kids are doing. I never gave a shit anyway. Why would I care if little Pomegranate or Pimento or Pinocchio or whatever his stupid name is can ride a bike now? I don't care if he can ride a unicycle and play Bach on the trumpet at the same time. And while I'm at it, why even come in the kitchen when I'm busy cooking for half of Wales and announce that? What were you thinking? 'Tam and Jan are in the kitchen working away getting Christmas lunch ready for everyone – I know, now would probably be a good time to go in there and start listing all my family's extraordinary achievements this year. They'll like that, I expect.'

It would take an effort of profound spiritual generosity on your part not to inwardly hip! hip! hooray! at the thought that this year you won't have to

> **Why would I care if little Pomegranate or Pimento or Pinocchio or whatever his stupid name is can ride a bike now?**

watch someone you actually hate guzzling your prized twenty-five-year-old malt. Who among us can truly claim that, upon learning Christmas was to be a quieter affair, they didn't sombrely express their deep disappointment, go to the bathroom, lock the door and break into a jig of pure joy?

It is interesting that you start with 'My problem is that I am really sick of Christmas.' Not even 'Hi Jack' or 'Hello, I wonder if you can help . . .' I don't point this out as a criticism; as a trained psychotherapist I welcome that level of directness and candour. I find that often, the very first thing a client says is the key to understanding him or her at a deeper level, which is why I always pay close attention to and appreciate their initial comments.*

Being 'really sick of Christmas', as you put it, is symptomatic of a mild depression that befalls many of us at some point in our lives. Probably for you, that point has been brought forward, turbo-charged by an excess of graft, stress and responsibility heaped upon you by circumstance. It occurs to me that you and your wife have been trying too hard to create the perfect experience and in so doing, have stopped enjoying the day yourselves. This is a very common mistake made by hosts at this time of the year. Only yesterday I was flicking through an interiors magazine – one of those glossies that are full of smart-arses banging on about how they always knit their own turkey and decorate the tree with real-life orphans holding candles, when I came across the following article by well-known designer Bulimia Silverspoon

---

* In this I obviously don't include opening remarks like 'Is it OK if I pay you next week?' and 'What kind of therapist has an office in the back room of a nail bar?' (That was a temporary arrangement, by the way.)

who said, 'One of my first jobs in November is to make the advent calendar. I like each day to reveal a small gift such as a piece of my homemade candied fruit or a tiny hand-stitched soft toy. It's such fun and you should see the children's faces when they open the little windows.' Right. And you, Bulimia, should be held in a secure darkened room for the duration of the festivities with whale music being played on a loop because that level of commitment to making others happy is dangerous and you need to be stopped for your own sake.

After all the hours of planning and hard work that you have put in to make Christmas a roaring success for everybody else, Tam, all you have been repaid with by your brother-in-law, that malingering ingrate, is his cheap shot Covid-based 'joke' aimed at your cooking. We can all be thankful that his quip was not actually delivered at the dining table. I have heard tell of a similar and, admittedly very badly timed, wisecrack that caused a fight at the table and resulted in the comedian having to actually swallow his paper crown to prevent himself from suffocating once it had been pushed down his throat.

You don't say if landing on your wife's family next year is an option but it is one solution in that it would give both of you the chance to spend time with them but without having to provide the catering and accommodation. The trouble with this is that it isn't really a long-term solution to your general disillusionment surrounding Christmas and their company. It also runs the risk of introducing an unwanted competitiveness that will only ramp up the pressure on you when it is your turn again. The last thing you need is a *Come Dine With Me*-style showdown in which marks are given and a winner announced. (No disrespect to *Come Dine With Me*. For the record, it is one of my favourite TV programmes and I will never tire of watching four clinically dim strangers trying to make conversation while not injuring themselves with the cutlery.)

You are right to have identified recent extraordinary events as an opportunity to review the Christmas custom that you have established of having everyone to your house. My worry, however, is that your in-laws do not strike me, from what you have said, as likely to read the mood. Some people can be very thick-skinned and you might quickly find yourself exhausted trying to pass hints in an effort to bring about the changes that you want. For example, starting the conversation casually with 'We were thinking maybe we might do something different this year for Christmas' ought to be enough to suggest that you want to make significant changes. But your wife's family will probably get the wrong end of the stick and reply with 'Oooh, great. What are you going to do for us, goose? I love goose. What a great idea. In fact I was getting a bit bored with your turkey. No offence.'

As you can see, this way, you will be back to square one, except it will be worse because you are now obliged to upgrade the menu. Best not to negotiate and risk ending up serving goose à la resentment; time to find a better way round the problem. So, given that there is a very realistic chance that you are stuck with hosting these people every Christmas for the rest of your life (sorry, but there's no point lying to you), I propose you adopt a system that serves me well. It's called cheating, and this is how it works:

Cheat with the cooking and forget trying to be Raymond

Blanc. You already know you can cook and you have nothing to prove, especially to this bunch of gannets. The point of the meal is that you and Jan enjoy it as much as possible and certainly as much as your guests. They've already shown their true colours with their snide, ungrateful swipes. So screw them.

Cheat with the turkey. Get one that is oven ready. No one needs to know you didn't spend all morning grinding chestnuts and grating oranges. They wouldn't care if you'd kidnapped Mary Berry and made her do it in the cellar. All they want is to stuff their faces and wash it down with as much sparkling as they can.

Cheat with the spuds. Buy them pre-done, stick them in one of your own dishes, keep schtum and enjoy watching their piggy little faces as they munch away at them. If they ask how you always get them so crispy, tap your nose and say it's a secret – which is true: a secret kept by whoever supplies tatties for the Mid Wales Frozen Food Co.

Cheat with the gravy, cheat with the sprouts, tell them you produced all the veg yourself (again true, if you include online shopping as a means of production), cheat with the bread sauce, cheat with the sodding red cabbage, tell them you made the crackers yourself if you want – they'll believe anything by now – and if you play Monopoly on Boxing Day, cheat at that as well. The net result will be the same: everyone got fed and watered, the difference being you didn't finish up wanting to start a major incident with the carving fork.

That's my advice anyway, Tam. I hope it helps, and if it isn't too early to say it: HAPPY CHRISTMAS!

My friend has just told me that she spotted my girlfriend on Tinder. I have to split up with her as I know I'll never be able to forgive her, but I thought she might have been The One. Any advice on how to mend a broken heart?

Try Tinder? It's working for her.

Four years ago I came to a crossroads in my life. Realising that I wasn't happy in my stressful, high-powered job in finance I took a leap and trained to become a secondary school teacher. I believed it would be fulfilling and that the hours and holidays would allow me more time with my wife and two children and that all of this would easily justify the significant salary cut that the career change entailed. Sadly, I have come to the conclusion that I made a mistake. Teaching is far and away the most stressful job I have ever had. The kids I teach are mostly rude and ungrateful and I am yet to meet another teacher at my school who likes his/her job.

The irony is that, although I probably do have more time with my own children than before, I now don't enjoy their company because of work. My wife has been supportive all along but agrees that the job has changed me. I really need to know what to do next and would appreciate your input.

Vihaan, Luton

Well, Vihaan, you are by no means the first teacher to have written that they have come to hate their job. Admittedly, the previous occurrences were all in my school reports in which I was routinely cited as the source of their disillusionment. By the time I left my secondary school, the headmaster calculated that I was pretty much directly responsible for the resignation or career change of five teachers. If you add in my maths teacher, whose mental-health crisis was blamed on me personally, that makes seven. (Obviously a joke. I do know that 5+1 = 6 but thought some well-judged humour would help at this point.)

For the record, the maths teacher in question, Clapper, or Mr Bell if we're going to be formal, was actually given early retirement (so, technically, we're back to five) after he attacked me in a fit of pique. Things reached boiling point towards the end of a double maths lesson as a result of one too many quips from yours truly. When Old Clappers asked the question: 'If I have twelve sweets in one pocket and nine sweets in the other, what do I have?' I piped up, 'Sir, a paedo's anorak, sir.' I can still remember my sense of pride quickly dissolving into horror when his bony, chalk-dusted hands clamped themselves around my neck as he screamed 'I'll fucking kill you, Dee, you stupid thick fuck. Christ, I fucking hate you . . .' People are sometimes critical of government school inspectors but I probably owe my life to the one who happened upon our classroom at that very moment and intervened. To this day I will never understand why, when I was the one nursing a bruised throat, not to mention probable shaken brain syndrome, Clappers got all the tea and sympathy and was driven home in a taxi.

Whether it is fair that I was blamed or not is another matter. The fact remains that it was a heavy burden for my young shoulders to bear. But bear it I have and it is one of many life experiences that has brought me to where I am today – helping people with their problems. It has been said that what doesn't kill you makes you stronger and I wholeheartedly agree. Of course there are caveats: an overdose of ketamine might not be fatal but will reduce you to spending the rest of your days wearing incontinence pants and watching *Countdown* from dawn till dusk. Yo, wossup rave dude? Vowel, please.

My observation is that your unhappiness is multilayered. You turn your back on a job in finance which you describe as stressful. Then when you arrive at your new teaching job, you discover that that is also stressful – in fact, more so. Lesson: work is stressful; that is why it's called work. It doesn't matter who you are or what it is you do for a living, this is a fact of life and it applies to every adult on the planet. OK, kids too if you include sportswear factories. If you have a job it means that you are doing something that someone else cannot or will not do and that is why you get paid – for taking stress from somebody else. Career choice becomes far less confusing once you accept this.

Now, some jobs are less stressful than others and that is one of the factors which determine rates of pay. By now you might be thinking that I am stating the obvious, but please reread the previous sentence, Vihaan, and I think that you will spot how misleading that statement is. Because the fact is, too often stress determines pay inversely. In other words, the most stressful jobs are frequently rewarded with the worst pay. For instance, I would say that being a nurse must be one of the most stressful jobs. Is it therefore, also one of the best paid jobs? Hardly. We all know that the opposite is true. So, then the argument goes something like, 'Yes, nursing is badly paid but it's rewarding, and that makes up for it.' True, nurses tend to be caring, kind individuals and, for that reason, get satisfaction from helping people who are ill. The trouble is that satisfaction won't pay the rent. A box of Quality Street from a recovered patient doesn't help your bank balance, but very few nurses are churlish enough to say 'Thanks, but keep your toffees, I'd prefer cash. I saved your life, you dickhead,' as I would. The financial pressure of a low-income occupation soon overwhelms the vocational rewards it might promise.

I give this example as it mirrors your experience with teaching. It has proved even more stressful than your previous life of gambling on foreign currencies or using other people's savings to buy and sell petrochemicals, corned beef, cluster bombs, PPE and Lord only knows what else. Yet, for the increased stress load, you have taken a sizeable pay cut. And unlike with a City job, you no longer get the chance to unwind of a Friday in a hotel room with a shovel-load of coke and a pair of strippers.

So now let's unpack the job satisfaction part of the dilemma. Of course there are teachers who find a profound sense of achievement from nurturing youngsters and guiding them towards a meaningful adulthood. Think of Mr Chips, Miss Jean Brodie or even Albus Dumbledore, for that matter. Admittedly, all fictional characters, but it is not entirely unimaginable that some real-life examples of contented teachers exist. The important fact here is that you, Vihaan, are not and never will be one of them. You have found that teaching sucks

> **And unlike with a City job, you no longer get the chance to unwind of a Friday in a hotel room with a shovel-load of coke and a pair of strippers**

and that you hate kids. Nobody is judging you for that. By the time children get to secondary school, they aren't even cute any more. We mostly know this from our own experience as parents. A child is a very special gift in anyone's life, but, when you think about it, it's only special because you don't actually know what it is until about fourteen years after you're given it. So it is that the gurgling bundle of love that you come home from the hospital with slowly, very slowly grows into a grunting malcontent and recreational drug user that you can hardly wait to leave home and go to university. Or anywhere. How would it be if you were given a Christmas present but weren't allowed to unwrap it for fourteen years? By that time you can't get a refund. You're stuck with something you don't really like and consigned to a life of pretending to be pleased with it.

Teaching is that same harsh experience magnified a thousand-fold. How could you ever be happy spending your life surrounded by gel-haired zit-pickers? Back in your old life you allowed yourself to indulge in the fantasy that, being a teacher, you would spend your days switching young minds on to education and the possibilities therein. You would be known as the teacher who made a difference, perhaps even the inspiration for a film about a guy who gives up a life of riches to dedicate himself to the betterment of otherwise hopeless youngsters. But it was just a dream and now you have been cruelly shaken awake by that merciless, cane-wielding pedagogue: reality.

These days your time at work is spent drearily preaching to rows of greasy hormone slaves who hate your guts and broodily think about how they'd like to torch your house. Preferably with you in it, chained to a radiator, by your nuts, so that to escape the flames you have to castrate yourself. God, I hated Mr Bell.

And, of course, all of this has impacted on your home life. You can no longer look at your own beloved children in the evening without seeing flashbacks of the zombies you're charged with teaching all day. It was better when you just came home from the office grumpy. Now you're hallucinating as well, like a soldier with PTSD. How long before you do a career-ending 'snap and lunge', like poor old Clapper? Will it be one of your kids or someone else's? Who knows?

You say your wife has been supportive and I am sure she has been. But everyone has their limits. Nobody can be expected to tolerate the demise of a partner without eventually cracking. Far be it from me to catastrophise, but I don't think it is unrealistic to imagine a day when you come back from school to discover the car has gone from outside your house. She and the kids will have gone to her mother's to 'think things over', leaving you with nothing but a Deliveroo menu and that bottle of Scotch your ex-boss gave you when you left.

It needn't come to that though, Vihaan. You have options. You asked for my input and here it is.

My favoured solution is you go to your ex-boss and say you want to come back. It will be humbling, but so is eating sandwiches in the common room for the rest of your life. Explain that you know it has been four years, but that it has been an invaluable learning curve and that you would be returning with a renewed skill set, not to say enthusiasm. Even if you have to accept a slightly lesser position than the one you left, say that you will enjoy the challenge of showing what a great addition you will be to the team with your newfound insight and energy. Don't try to style it out either. Be honest about the fact that you screwed up and show a willingness to laugh out loud at your ridiculous decision. Go in expecting hostility but knowing that it is nothing compared to what you have had to put up with from those wankers you have been trying to teach.

Supposing a return to your original company is not possible, don't despair. Go to your GP and get a sick note (tell her you're a teacher, she'll understand) so that you can spend time chasing leads and going to interviews. Unless there is something you haven't disclosed in your letter – like the real reason you left the City was you got prosecuted for embezzlement – then I think you have a good chance of clawing back the life that you so recklessly tossed aside in a moment of altruistic madness.

However, should none of this come to pass and you discover that the corporate world you abandoned has changed the locks and won't answer the phone, then it might be that you will have to resign yourself to teaching. If this is the case, my suggestion would be as follows: stop caring.

Of all the people I know who have survived the profession, every one of them has told me that the secret is to jettison all the good intentions you went into teaching with and become a cynical, callous bastard who trudges through each term on his weary way towards their pension. This way, your pupils' indifference – nay, hatred towards you – will barely even register. Never again will you go home demoralised and broken by a bunch of acne-splattered ingrates, because you gave them no cause to be grateful in the first place. It's a zero-sum game. Go home to your wife and children, invigorated by the knowledge that you set out that day to do precisely nothing to enhance anybody's life and that you succeeded.

Good luck, Vihaan, and I hope that I have been able to help you untangle some of the issues that I believe have been bringing you unnecessary distress.

Dear Jack. My husband Ron and I have been married for 9 years and have two young children. We don't argue particularly, but ever since the children were born, we're just parents, Mum and Dad, and there is no romance in our lives any more. We sleep in separate beds and lead separate lives unless it involves the children. Should we separate now or wait until the children have established their own lives at university?

Dawn, Wrexham
(I have changed our names for reasons of anonymity)

Dawn, thank you for your email and I am happy that you have changed 'your' and 'Ron's' names. Even happier that you did it in such an intelligent way. I recently had a letter from a man whose life was made difficult due to an uncontrollable night-time fetish which involved secretly defecating in people's gardens around the village where he lived. He finished the letter by saying that he was writing under a false name as he didn't want everyone knowing his business. Sometimes it's hard to keep a straight face in this job. Not when it comes to your problem, however.

Many couples lose their way and go to strenuous lengths to convince their children that it is not their fault that Mum and Dad aren't going to live together any more. But it is not an accident that you have unequivocally identified your children's arrival as a massively negative turning point in your marriage. In my view, far too few children get given the full low-down when they ask about their parents' separation. This is a mistake because, let's face it, of course it's the kids' fault and telling them otherwise only prompts them towards a lifetime of causing emotional havoc wherever they go with total impunity.

Much better when they ask why you separated to gently explain. 'Well, son,' you might begin, if you've watched too much American television, 'we used to be a very happy couple but, looking back, I can see that much of that was dependent on us being able to get sufficient sleep and privacy, or eat without having yoghurt and bits of fish fingers thrown at us, being able to go for a walk without having to carry 3 stone of writhing, screaming infant under one arm and a trike under the other, being able to look round a shop without someone whining about wanting a drink or a biscuit or to go wee-wees, being able to drink a cup of coffee without having to make mindless chat about sodding Square Pants Flannel Bob or whatever his fucking name was, being able to enjoy a glass of wine without it being sent flying because you thought that would be a good time to run in and show off your lassoing skills, and being able to listen to Neil Young in the car and not that medicated freak Barney the Dinosaur singing about bloody friendship and kindness to the point where you just want to slam your foot down and drive into a brick wall at 70mph. The health of our marriage depended on all those things, you see, and once those things were denied us, we soon realised that we no longer had a viable relationship because we no longer had a life. And so we decided to split for the sake of our sanity and the highly attractive prospect that, although we'll miss each other sometimes, at least we'll get every other weekend off from you.'

When you have spoken, don't forget to comfort your child with, 'But what's really important is you mustn't blame yourself, OK?' or some other reassurance. Obviously this last bit is untrue, but advisable to cover yourself in the future. Kids tend not to take being directly blamed for the destruction of their family unit very maturely. At the very least, they will mull it over for the next forty years or so then let rip at a family wedding with a drunken rant – 'You never really wanted me. All you ever bloody cared about was yourself . . .' – not the speech everyone was expecting.

However, let's not get too far ahead of ourselves. It's important to remember that the situation described above is merely hypothetical in your case because you are not yet at a stage where a break-up is unavoidable.

It's a mistake to believe that you can schedule emotional pain – that it can be neatly timed

Adjusting to a three-year stretch studying lawnmower maintenance at Luton University instead of the hoped-for pure mathematics at Imperial College will take time

to coincide with the kids leaving home. Furthermore, you should not delude yourself that entry to university triggers any kind of maturity. If anything, freshers are still processing the PTSD brought on by the unexpectedly harsh workload of A levels and then ending up at their second choice anyway. Adjusting to a three-year stretch studying lawnmower maintenance at Luton University instead of the hoped-for pure mathematics at Imperial College will take time. The last thing he or she needs at that juncture is bad news from the nest. Even if things go well and they get to their chosen university, much of the first year will be a haze of excessive drug taking, group sex and public humiliation. And that's just the hockey team initiation. Believe me, your children will need security and support at this stage, perhaps more so than at any other. Remember, they have just left home and will have compromised stress immunity brought on by a diet of cider, weed and Pot Noodles. It would be disastrous for them if, at a time when they are tentatively venturing into the foothills of adulthood, they learn of their parents' intended split. Not to mention the sense of betrayal: the knowledge that entry to university was seen by you not as the pinnacle of achievement but as a planned deadline for dismantling everything they know.

The next thing to say is that from what I deduce from your letter, relations between you and Ron are absolutely not beyond repair. So, you don't really talk to each other or do anything together and you sleep in separate beds – granted, that is not promising. But when you look at it optimistically – and as you know, I am very much a glass half full type of person – these issues are common in many marriages. It's just that you have achieved all this forty years too soon and you have done it without the atrophying effect of a disappointing life and general tetchiness.

As an onlooker, albeit one with considerable expertise and powers of perception, I would say that the first step you need to take is to examine the lethargy that has taken hold in your relationship. 'We don't argue particularly' is a choice of wording that worries me. It flags up an emotional laziness between the two of you. When we argue, it is because we care about our views in the context of our partner's opinion. By contrast, you don't care what Ron thinks and the feeling is mutual. I suggest that you start to engage with each other in conversations and activities, but with the expectation that this will lead to disagreements and arguments. My hunch is that it will clear the air and you will both begin to feel stimulated by the sense that you matter to each other. Get someone to look after the kids so that the two of you can go to the cinema together, then go for a drink or even a meal and talk. Not about your relationship, but about the film you've just seen. If you agree with what Ron says, tell him. If you don't, enjoy the debate. These 'date nights' could become the building blocks of a new accord between you both.

Yes, this might be difficult at first. You might learn details about each other that are unexpected and require new levels of understanding from and about both of you. You might realise shortly after Ron begins his in-depth film review that he is a monumental bore. He might use the occasion to tell you that he is, say, massively in debt, thinking of getting a greenhouse to grow tomatoes in, addicted to prescription drugs, a secret cross-dresser who wants to be called Cynthia and longs to go shopping for frocks with you, has become a Scientologist, wants you both to learn scuba-diving or ballroom dancing, a Russian agent known as Dmitry sent here to stoke civil disorder in Wrexham (I'm in), or that he is in fact a plain-clothes cop called Kev who married you and had children with you as a cover because all along, he has been investigating your neighbours for unpaid parking tickets dating back to 2004. Who knows what might emerge? Don't worry about it. It's a process of buying some time so that you can really explore what to do next and how to progress your relationship. If the truth doesn't set you free, it might at least release you on parole. Having reached the separate bed stage I suspect it's going to take more than a weepy at the flicks and a bucket of *vinho verde* at Nando's to relight the fire but you owe it to yourselves to give it a try.

Frankly you have nothing to lose. If you can make a fresh start then you will have saved yourself and your family a world of grief. And if you just can't get along with Cynthia – sorry, Dmitry, Kev, no – Ron – then you will at least know you did your best but in the end walked away from an irredeemably broken marriage. All the best, Dawn, and I hope I have helped.

Is there a god?

If there is, I suggest switching him off and back on again.

Dear Jack, my 28-year-old son won't leave home. He has had a good education and now has a well-paid job. However, he says that it suits him to be living with me. I am a divorcee and ideally would like to meet somebody new to share my life with, but I can't see that happening with this ongoing situation.

Karen, Southend

The first thing to say is that you are not alone by any stretch of the imagination. Just google it and you'll see the scale of the problem. Not that Google can be trusted on this, considering it is entirely staffed by twenty-eight-year-olds who haven't left home and spend all day in an HQ that is less like an office and more like a sprawling playpen with swings, slides and ball pits like some kind of *Teletubbies* theme park, albeit not quite as creepy. It's incredible to me that Silicon Valley haven't made it mandatory for employees to come to work in romper suits, gliding along on electric scooters, dummies in mouth. Of course, there are those who would argue that there is a time and a place for adults to rediscover their inner child and I would agree with them. It's just that that time and place usually involves a dingy basement flat, a grumpy sex worker and adult-size nappies.

Back to your son and why he won't leave home. The crux of the problem is that he probably can't. Let's take a look at the reasons why that might be.

1. He can't move out because property prices are astronomical and show no sign of coming down significantly any time soon. Even if you have a good job, as you say your son has, it is incredibly hard for young people to get onto the property ladder. And by that I mean being able to buy your first house or flat. It's a term worth clarifying as in some circles 'property ladder' means the thing you use if you're a burglar. Too many films and TV dramas romanticise burglars as lithe, acrobatic types dressed in black who skilfully straddle and limbo their way through alarmed laser beams in pursuit of priceless quarry from a billionaire's mansion; or abseil from a roof light to surgically remove a museum piece from its plinth – artists of larceny for whom no security system is too great a challenge. Who can honestly say that they would resent being burgled by anyone with such elan? If someone goes to that much trouble to break in, they can have my Seiko. They're welcome to it, in fact. It was a gift, and a bit blingy to my eye. Whenever I put it on I feel a strange urge to sell PPI to someone. If it got stolen by a professional thief I'd merely be losing a cheap Japanese watch and gaining an anecdote – '. . . *apparently the police have nicknamed her Catwoman. Anyway, they think she used a rope and grappling hook to swing across to our upstairs window from next door, then she unlocked the window with a miniature drill. We didn't hear a thing. She only took the Seiko but left a small gold card imprinted with the silhouette of a panther.*'

2. Bring on the gritty TV drama I say – probably from Scandinavia – that dares to tell the truth about robberies, albeit in subtitles: a tough but likeable cop with a drink problem investi-

gates a bog-standard break-in. Some high-as-a-kite crackhead has jemmied the back door with an iron bar, trashed the living room, nicked the Sky box and taken a dump on the coffee table. Right on the doily, in fact.

3. Apologies for the detour, Karen. However, I wanted to be quite sure that everybody understands the crucial difference between aspiring to own a property and breaking into a property. You have to remember that other people from Southend might be reading this as well.

4. He can't move out because, even if he had the deposit, he can't get a mortgage. Up until 2008 mortgages were given out like leaflets at an arts festival. Obviously the similarity doesn't end there as most mortgages have low interest as well. Seriously, there was very little paperwork involved and when you were required to fill in a form, you certainly didn't have to be honest. Nobody was going to check that you really earned as much as you claimed, or even that you actually were the 'top barrister' that you claimed to be. It was all done with a nudge and a wink, completed over a couple of cans of Amstel, signed in crayon, witnessed by the bloke who works at Londis and sold you the Amstel, stuffed in the post and two weeks later you had your offer. Two hundred grand, thank you very much, and bye-bye Mummy. Looking back, it's hard to imagine how such a fail-safe system that underpinned the entire Western economy went so terribly wrong.

5. He can't move out because renting is so expensive. This is likely to be the gist of many a conversation that you and your son have had. But looked at from another angle, he can't move

out because blagging a room off you is irresistibly cheap, convenient and secure. We love our children, which is why we nearly always do too much for them. Some might implore you to get tough with your boy, turf him out, let him learn at the University of Hard Knocks. Well, I am a UHK alumnus (although back then it was only a polytechnic – another cross for me to bear) and I can tell you it isn't all it's cracked up to be. I took resentment studies with modules in bitterness and jealousy. Naturally I gained a first and was tempted to do a master's in self-pity, but fate took me on a different course. My point is that it was only when I was clear of that negative mindset that I was able to emerge as the ball of positive energy whose words you are now reading.

> **Naturally I gained a first and was tempted to do a master's in self-pity, but fate took me on a different course**

Whichever reason is behind his unwillingness to move out, perhaps your son requires some extra support at this time. Maybe life seems insurmountably bleak for him. Maybe he hasn't even really got a job. What if the truth is that he spends every day sitting around in the local shopping centre flicking bits of paper into the fountain that doesn't work any more, occasionally wandering into Clintons and reading the humour-section greetings cards? Or perhaps he really does have a job, but the idea of committing so much of his income to a solution that is worse than the problem is deeply unappealing? Leaving home is hard and, ideally, he would have done so by now for both your sakes but, given the options, why would he? Why wrench himself from the, admittedly, slothful comfort of familiarity and trade it for some bleak, vacated room above a laundrette? There is nothing remotely exciting about the prospect of sleeping on an unknown mattress that smells as if someone has died on it. Especially when you eventually learn from the owner of the laundrette that it smells that way because someone *has* died on it.

Hopefully, the problem will resolve itself and one morning in the near future your son will casually mention that he and a couple of friends have found a flat to share and are going to give it a go. You will find yourself almost resenting the blasé manner in which he has overlooked the stress he has caused you these past few years but eventually you will come to see it as looking after an injured bird that never even looked back when it finally flew away. You did what you knew you needed to do and he just did what he is designed to do.

At about the same time you will begin to miss his company. Home will not feel like home without his abandoned clothes on the hall floor and the detritus of a recent fry-up in the kitchen. That is when you will write to me again to tell of the darkening sense of loneliness that shadows you every day. And I will be there for you, Karen, always ready to shine my light into your life. Until we speak again, good luck.

> *My dog never wants to hang out with me, only with my boyfriend.*
> *How do I undermine their bond to become the firm favourite?*
>
> Louise, South Wales

You have done the right thing by asking for help, Louise. There are some practical steps that I think you can take in order to remedy this sad situation but I also want to discuss the insecurity you are feeling, which seems to be the underlying issue.

As the saying goes, 'A dog is a man's best friend' and this is certainly true here. The problem being that, in this case, the dog was supposed to be your best friend but has decided that you don't make the grade.

Louise, you will not be the first person to realise that letting a dog into their life is a terrible mistake. Many others have reached this conclusion for themselves. Take, for example, this typical scenario.

Our prospective dog owner is called Stuart. Stuart and his partner Lyndsey have a two-year-old daughter, Coleen, who never fails to point at any dog she sees and then say 'doggy'. The first time this happened, Stuart and Lyndsey found it rather sweet that their daughter was so excited by seeing a dog. Then it happened again a few minutes later, on the same walk but with a different dog. Just as she uttered her twentieth repetition of 'doggy, doggy, doggy, doggy', another dog appeared and so the monotone chanting started up again. During the course of an hour-long walk, Coleen might have seen thirty or so dogs and each one she greeted with a seemingly longer and longer litany. To the point, in fact, that the young parents wished they had a sheet that they could drape over the pushchair in order to stop Coleen from seeing any more dogs. By the time they were an hour into the walk, Stuart had stormed off back to the car and Lyndsey had started smoking again.

The young couple began to dread walks and certainly avoided meeting up with their friends from NCT, all of whose children appeared able to see a dog without it prompting the irritating refrain. On one occasion, a friend suggested that Coleen obviously had an affinity with dogs and that Stuart and Lyndsey ought to nurture this. In actual fact, the friend was just being nice and made the suggestion to stop herself saying that she thought Coleen was clearly deranged. Nevertheless, the couple took the idea to heart.

And so, as you might by now be guessing, this is when the difficulties began. The couple were sold a pup and found themselves at the threshold of finding out just what that expression means.

After twenty minutes in the car on their way home with the new dog, Lyndsey remarked how curious it was that Coleen, strapped into her Mothercare seat in the back was gazing out of the window, evincing no interest at all and having not uttered the word 'doggy' a single time. Could the ploy of buying the child a dog to stop her saying 'doggy' the whole time have worked? But then Coleen spoke. When the car stopped at some lights, she had spotted a cat idly lying on a wall and she said – you guessed it – 'cat'. This she repeated continuously until, a few weary miles later, she poked her little fingers into the puppy's travel cage, received a playful but no doubt quite painful bite and screamed non-stop for the rest of the day.

A week later and 'Covid' – as they had decided to call the dog once it was clear that he was going to be nearly impossible to control and would always need to wear a muzzle in public spaces – had probably doubled in size, although his cold beady eyes appeared to be shrinking into his skull like something you might see painted on a Hell's Angel's motorbike. Having only recently got Coleen sleeping through the night, it seemed doubly unfair to Stuart and Lyndsey that Covid did not like sleeping in the kitchen and showed his objection at about 2 a.m. with a wretched howling that continued until he was allowed up into their bedroom, where he would try to engage them in a rough sort of play by tearing at their duvet, all the while signalling his dominance with rancid emissions of wind.

Within six months, the couple had become bleary and fractious. Covid was a bad sleeper and determined that his owners should follow suit. His initial puppyish yap had given way to a deafening and menacingly deep bark that conjured the image of Gestapo raids. Exercising the beast had to be limited to late-night sorties when there were fewer joggers, cyclists and quick-moving (not quick enough, as it transpired) children to excite Covid into attack mode. As a result, house-training was all but aborted and the muscly 54-kilo adult dog felt at liberty to discharge wherever, whenever and whatever he wanted.

With most of the carpets in the house ruined with urine and the back lawn now a turd minefield, life had become unmanageable in the extreme. At one point, Stuart even googled 'how to kill a dog' but lost his nerve when he realised that Covid was staring over his shoulder at the screen and starting to growl aggressively. Locking himself in the bathroom, Stuart used his phone to find out where the nearest dog home was located. That afternoon, without the slightest remorse, he presented at the rescue centre gates with Covid and told the story of how he had found the poor thing abandoned on the dual carriageway near his house. He would, swore Stuart, have given the dog a home himself were it not for the fact that his daughter is an asthmatic. And that was that. Covid was eventually rehomed, given a very long chain and an unlicensed scrap metal yard in the Midlands to guard, where he could assault council inspectors, the police and other trespassers with impunity.

> **At one point, Stuart even googled 'how to kill a dog' but lost his nerve when he realised that Covid was staring over his shoulder at the screen**

All of which, Louise, is to show that your predicament is far from unusual. Like Stuart and Lyndsey, the simple mistake that you made was believing that you could easily control your dog's behaviour and allegiances. Look at the plus side. Your dog is capable of affection, even if he doesn't show it to *you*. You get to own a dog but your boyfriend will feel duty bound to look after it. Think of your boyfriend and dog as a package: a 'two for the price of one' deal. Accept that such deals are rarely satisfactory or even wanted. A bit like when you buy a paperback at a railway station and they offer you a second one free, thus forcing you to miss your train while you search in vain for just one more book in the whole shop that's not unacceptably crap.

My point is that not everyone welcomes getting more than he or she bargained for. But what's done is done. The way forward, in this case, is to accept that this is the situation and that it can work to your advantage. Please don't think you have to debase yourself to regain your boyfriend's affections. All that is required is a little bit of patience on your behalf. Face it, he is unwittingly showing preference for a companion who sometimes drinks from the lavatory. It won't take very long for this habit alone to drop in status from 'Instagram cute' to 'vomit inducing'. Similarly, your boyfriend will begin to miss the days when he would wake up to your dreamy eyes and petal-scented breath rather than a trout-sized tongue lathering his face with Chum dribble.

Best of luck, Louise, and I hope things work out for you.

> *Lockdown has turned me into a nosy neighbour, a real curtain twitcher. Help!*
>
> *Jan, Hungerford*

Well, Jan, as I write this, we are currently experiencing national levels of anxiety not experienced since Garry Glitter returned from Thailand.

Living with stress, as we all have been doing, can change the way that we normally behave, so, first of all, you should stop feeling bad if you find yourself constantly prying and judging your neighbours as they go about their daily business. And stress reveals much about a person's true personality – are we, as individuals in difficult situations, likely to cope or be overwhelmed? (Or, in your case, to obsessively keep tabs on next door and grass them up for having a barbecue etc.)

Many of us in lockdown have discovered new ways of passing time. These have tended to revolve around traditional hobbies and crafts – knitting suddenly became more popular than it deserves to be. Sometimes these activities have created their own tensions. For example, I cannot be the only person in the country to have tired very slightly of stories about bread baking. A pandemic is not an excuse to start showing off. Your local artisan baker is having enough difficulty keeping his business going through this crisis without having to compete with smug furloughees endlessly shovelling out batches of loaves and giving them away to anyone they half know. In addition to this, they fully expect the same baker to freely supply them with sourdough starter because of an article in one of the Sunday papers in which a well-known food writer merrily suggested that artisan bakers are only too happy to provide this service. It's a testament to the forbearance of those same bakers that the NHS was not further burdened by hundreds of emergency patients requiring treatment for Kilner-jar-related injuries. (Indeed, it was the same food writer who previously advised me, via her column, that if I wasn't sure how to fillet and bone my own sea bass, to 'Just ask your local fishmonger to do it for you and he'll be glad to oblige.' Wrong. My fishmonger was not glad to oblige and wondered, out loud, whether I wanted him to 'cook and eat the f***ing thing as well'. Some people in the queue found this amusing, others tried to suppress their glee but I can still tell a smirk even if it is covered by a PPE mask.)

Please be reassured that you live in a country that is renowned for its common sense and pragmatism; thus its citizens will only ever breach lockdown regulations under exceptional circumstances. These occur infrequently but might include the weather turning warm, your football team winning a big match or seeing a statue that you want to pull down.

You are not Mata Hari, you are Jan from Hungerford. But for whatever reason, your lockdown hobby has been snooping on your neighbours to make sure that they are not behaving in a way that could endanger members of the public. Although unpalatable to most people, this has given you a sense of fulfilment and the feeling that you are being proactive in the fight against coronavirus. Unfortunately, this low-level meddling is gradually evolving into a more sinister form of neighbourhood spying, the likes of which generally disappeared along with the Berlin Wall. Without wishing to exaggerate, what you characterise as being a 'curtain twitcher' is in fact the same insidious behaviour that has propped up every tyrannical regime throughout history. It is essential that you rein in your impulses and cease this snooping. So what if next door had a laugh in their garden cooking some bangers and drinking Prosecco? So bloody what?

> **Unfortunately, this low-level meddling is gradually evolving into a more sinister form of neighbourhood spying, the likes of which generally disappeared along with the Berlin Wall**

Think of them as the resistance fighters of our age, bravely rallying against a merciless virus by continuing to show good cheer in the face of terror. Join them, Jan. Get word to them somehow that you are willing to help. It is time to raise your head above the parapet – or, in your case, garden fence – and confide that your sympathies lie with them and that you have a chilled bottle of Sauvignon and you're not afraid to use it.

> *My wife has suggested we have a threesome with another woman.*
> *We haven't got to the details of who yet but I'm not keen. Does this*
> *make me weird? And if not, how do I break it to her?*
>
> *(Via SMS)*

I suspect what she really wants is a twosome with another woman which, ironically, is what you'll probably both end up with anyway.

> *Hi Jack, I have been living with my girlfriend for the last year and she won't marry me. I feel rejected by this and wonder if there is a future in our relationship if she can't commit.*
>
> *Marcus, Stoke*

In the past a lethal combination of societal compulsion, peer pressure, family expectation and a general lack of concentration has led millions of women down the aisle to the altar of loveless union. Freed from such coercions, your girlfriend has given herself the space and time to make an informed choice: a kind of 'try before you buy, money back if not delighted scheme'. She has kept the receipt in a safe place because deep down she knows she might have her doubts about you.

A year is ample time to grow weary of somebody's personality. It's one reason Doctor Who metamorphoses so frequently. Even those traits which at first made you attractive to your girlfriend have now lost their appeal. For example, the tone of your question suggests a level of anxiety on your part. Let us suppose that she originally found this an endearing quality in you. Imagine for a minute that it was reassuring that you were not the usual louche, cock-sure gym stud she had likely encountered in the past and that she found it refreshing to meet a man who was, say, constantly self-questioning, passive and prone to anxiety attacks in social situations. But what if after a few weeks it began to grate that you were always such a wimp? That your insistence on surrendering your own wishes in order to accommodate hers became unbearable? (HER: 'How do you want your tea?' YOU: 'I really don't mind, I'm easy' – that kind of thing. Seen like this it's amazing she never threw the kettle at you.)

She might start to feel as though you were trying to suffocate her with your indifference. It wouldn't all be your fault, of course. How could either of you fully appreciate that you were a rebound boyfriend anyway? Yes, her ex was indeed a louche, cock-sure gym stud but his innate attractiveness would now also become apparent every time she came home to find you listening to Dido and baking cupcakes. From there, it would be no great leap of logic to conclude that you are not a keeper and that she needs to confide this to her friends, family, colleagues and all her followers on TikTok. Everyone except you, actually.

> **Where she clearly sees herself as vibrant, sensual and eager for life, she sees you as the opposite, someone completely void of hope or self-respect with a permanent expression of despair, like a stamped-on pie**

Of course, this is all speculation, but you have to think that, were it true, she would doubtless be wondering what on earth you would become after several years/decades together if you were already behaving like a scolded houseboy, secretly sending weepy missives to the likes of yours truly. Surely time will not embolden or favour you. Rather, as the decades roll by like tumbleweed, she may well fear you will slowly shrink to a point of non-existence. Where she clearly sees herself as vibrant, sensual and eager for life, she sees you as the opposite, someone completely void of hope or self-respect with a permanent expression of despair, like a stamped-on pie.

The simple fact is that marriage is no longer the natural and expected end result of a relationship. While there are many social and cultural reasons for this, the important one is that it is no longer considered shameful to be living out of wedlock with someone with whom you are in a relationship. Another is that of parents utterly hating the person their daughter lives with, but perhaps that's just my imagination adding unnecessary complications for you to lose sleep over.

Really, the time has come for you to revisit your own thoughts on marriage and why it is so important to you. There are deep and profound reasons for getting married, such as tax exemptions, but wanting it as an assurance of your partner's commitment shouldn't be one of them. With a little introspection I would not be surprised if you were to conclude that, in fact, marriage is not relevant to you or the continuation of your relationship; even that your desire for it is actually a voicing of your insecurity.

The only caveat I would include is that you do not alter your attitude too dramatically or suddenly. In other words, don't swing from 'Marry me, please marry me. I adore you. You're the love of my life. Marry me' one day, to the next saying, 'You know what, I've been thinking about us and I'm not that bothered about marrying you anyway so let's just leave things as they are and drift. You do your thing, I'll do my thing and who knows what will happen? We marry, we don't marry, we stay together, we break up. Who cares? Not me.' Too radical an approach might spook your girlfriend altogether and even confirm, in her mind, the false notion that you are weak, indecisive and unreliable and therefore bad husband material. Relationships fall apart for many reasons, Marcus; don't let irony be one of them. I hope this has helped in some small way – and good luck.

> Hello Jack, for some time now my best friend Katya and I have wanted to start a small business. We did consider making and selling face masks but feel that this is a bad business model because demand will disappear once there is a vaccine. Both of us are keen on cooking and thought about producing a range of pickles and chutneys that we could sell online and then in supermarkets, but initial results have not been encouraging. We feel that we are very ideas-orientated and that with the right inspiration have it in us to make a success of something. Have you any suggestions that might point us in the right direction? Any input from you at this stage would be much appreciated.
>
> Susanne, East Sussex

Hi Susanne. This is an unusual email for me to receive given that you are asking for practical business advice rather than emotional guidance. However, I am interested to explore what you have said because so often an apparently unconnected issue in our life (in your case wanting to start your own business) is, in fact, related to our psychological profile. One question that we might need to address is whether your ambition is likely to be aided or thwarted by your personality. On first appearance, the statement 'for some time now my best friend Katya and I have wanted to start a small business' is positive and points to someone with energy, vitality and a dynamic approach to the world. Looked at forensically, however, something different comes into focus. This often happens in psychotherapy. It's a bit like one of those Magic Eye pictures that you look at and look at and suddenly it transforms from a pattern of squirls into a picture of a shark. Although, for me personally, it never worked. I even bought a book of Magic Eye art in order to experience the weird illusions for myself, having heard so much about them. After at least an hour of staring at the pages I was convinced I had been ripped off, took the book back to the shop and asked for a refund. I won't use these pages to fully describe the argument I got into at the bookshop because, frankly I'm bigger than that. Suffice to say it went something like this:

ME: I bought this Magic Eye book here yesterday, but none of the patterns work, so I'd like a refund, please.

SHOP OWNER: So you've read the book?

ME: No, I haven't read the book. There is nothing to read. I just looked at all the pictures and, like I say, they don't work. I didn't see any mermaids, no Empire State Buildings, no seagulls, no tractors. There's nothing hidden in any of them ... So can I please have my money—

SHOP OWNER: (interrupting): This isn't a library. It's a shop. You can't buy a book, read it and then bring it back asking for—

ME: I didn't read it, did I?

SHOP OWNER: Please don't shout at me.

ME (*quietly and politely*): I'm not shouting . . .

SHOP OWNER: You were shouting, actually . . .

Another man enters from the back room of the shop.

OTHER MAN: Is everything all right, Michael? I heard
   shouting.

SHOP OWNER: Everything is fine, thank you, Paul. This
   gentleman was asking for a refund and I was explaining
   that since he has read, sorry, looked at all the pictures
   in the book, he can't expect us to take it back.

ME: You're making it sound like a children's book—

SHOP OWNER (*interrupting again*): It is actually from the
   Under-Tens section.

OTHER MAN: What is wrong with the book anyway?

ME: Oh for fu— Look, if you stare at these pictures they're
   supposed to turn into something else and they don't.
   OK? They just don't. The book is not fit for purpose.
   It doesn't work, probably never did. It's broken. Call
   it what you want, I want my money back. All right?

OTHER MAN: Did you just swear at me?

THE END.

Or, not actually THE END. In fact, the discussion became
quite heated because of their attitude, not helped by another
customer in the shop chipping in that I should try a book with
words as well as pictures, holding up a children's reader called
The Fearless Octopus. 'Look,' he said, pointing at the illustration
on the cover, 'there's a picture of an octopus you *can* see.' How
hilarious. And what a clever way to defuse a tense situation.

Not. At that point I did shout and swear. I shouted and swore to such an extent that any fair-minded person who had been there would have had to admit that my previous denials of shouting and swearing should be upheld. Anyway, I didn't get my refund and, needless to say, Susanne, I won't be going back there any time soon. And not just because I've been banned.

I apologise for the detour, but I think it will have been worthwhile if it reminds us to look closely at the true meaning of our words. To recap, then, you said 'for some time now my best friend Katya and I have wanted to start a small business'. Immediately 'for some time now . . .' tells me that you are in a state of inertia, unable to progress from the initial fleeting thought that you would like to start a business. It is as if the very thought of all the work that that would involve has floored you before you even got the stationery printed. There is no point in having ideas if you don't act upon them. Just imagine if Paul McCartney had left forming a band at the idea stage. He'd just be an old guy in a Merseyside pub getting sozzled on vegetarian beer and telling anyone who'll listen, 'Me and my mate John had this idea we'd start a band and call it the Beatles and write all these songs that would change music forever. But you know, for various reasons we didn't crack on with it and things just didn't work out that way. I got a job in a carpet factory and I've got my pension now so I can't complain.' Other regulars would learn to avoid him, or at least cut him off mid songwriting rant with a poignantly ironic 'Yeah, yeah, yeah.'

It is a terrifying thought that you might already have missed your big break by procrastinating, which is why the true entrepreneur is a restless, impulsive beast, always desperate to move forward for fear of wasting any opportunity.

Perhaps I'm even more worried by the end of your sentence where you say you want to 'start a small business'. Nobody successful set out on their journey wanting 'small'. Nobody. Did James Dyson dream of selling dusters? Did Jeff Bezos excitedly blurt out: 'I've got it! Online retail is the future and I want to be part of it. Mum, Dad, I'm going to be a van driver!' Or did Bill Gates ever say he wanted to invent a special typewriter that occasionally just randomly stops working and loses everything you've written? OK, maybe Bill got his wish, but you can see where I'm going, can't you? Don't think 'small'.

Nobody successful set out on their journey wanting 'small'. Nobody

Now I'd like to raise the question of what Katya is doing in all of this. Am I missing something here, or is she a dead weight? I can't see what she is bringing to the picnic. Yes, she's your best friend but if things go to plan (and with my help I think they will), you'll soon be incredibly successful and rich and will have a more exciting social life than you ever imagined. It's often said that it's lonely at the top but it's rarely appreciated that this is because you must abandon everyone who cares about you as you make for the summit, and that base camp is littered with the bodies of best friends. I say ditch Katya. And do it soon, before she holds you back any more.

That sounds harsh, perhaps, but if I am not right, it is only because I got the two of you the wrong way round and that Katya is the inspired one who secretly wants you out so that she can get on and make a go of things. In which case, really the same advice applies. Only to her.

Either way, it's surely better you find these things out by heeding my words. The alternative is to blindly stagger on until one of you collapses under the stress of having to see each other every day. Or, worse still, you are forced to confront your flawed friendship on the BBC's *Dragons' Den* when it clearly and obviously doesn't fare well under the scrutiny of five multimillionaire psychopaths. Normally it is a comfort to have someone standing by your side in a testing situation, but that particular crucible of sadism can destroy even lifelong friendships.

Imagine it, you've made your pitch with only one or two fluffed lines and you've even answered their opening question impressively. OK, the question was 'Where are you from?' but it's a start. You hold it together even when the first couple of rejections fly in like guided missiles: 'Here's where I am, Susanne and Katya. I'm going to be honest with you. I don't think you have a business here, I think you're a couple of useless fuckwits and I'd rather eat my own shit than get involved with either of you and your bollocks idea, and for that reason, I'm out.' (The other one is unprintable.)

But then, just as self-doubt begins to creep in and you start to think that there really is no future in clogs made from recycled muesli, the melodrama ratchets up a notch. That one who plays with her pen the whole time says, 'I'm going to make you an offer. I'm going to offer you half the money but I want

90 per cent of the business, the deeds to your house, one of your kidneys, the family photo album your mum left you and the right hand of your first-born as a key fob.' It's a bit more than you ideally wanted to give away. You ask if you can have a moment to discuss it and your request is duly granted. You are up for trying to haggle the dragon down to 80 per cent and go from there but Katya is sickened and totally against the deal on principle and even whispers something about involving Ofcom or at least contacting the tabloids. It's then that you realise how badly you have misjudged your so-called business partner. Turns out she hasn't got the stomach for wheeler-dealing and you're the one with the acumen, the drive and determination needed to get to the top. Much better you make these discoveries about your friendship in private than on a TV show where you can't even attack each other in the lift afterwards without it being filmed.

Next, I think we should look at the ideas that you mentioned and what we can learn about you from them. Surprisingly, you decided that face-mask manufacturing was unpromising. This during a time when every government in the Western world was awarding generous contracts to anyone who could so much as UHU two bits of string to a tissue. Even if you prove to be right, surely one thing that we are all getting used to is the realisation that, as a species, we are biologically fallible and share a future of new restrictions and imposed safeguards. There is no reason at all to believe that after a certain date in the near future, all forms of PPE will suddenly become redundant. Quite the opposite. Getting in on the face-mask industry at the beginning of

2020 could well have been a very smart move, leading to years of robust sales. Instead, you talked yourselves out of it like someone who thinks she won't run for that bus in case she still doesn't reach the stop in time. It makes zero sense and neatly fulfils its own fear.

The same can't be said for chutney, which to my knowledge, has never enjoyed a boom in demand unless you count the advent of the ploughman's lunch, but even that was negligible thanks to the pointlessly small ramekin it was portioned into. And yet, again the idea was abandoned within moments of being alighted upon. You don't go into detail when you say that 'initial results have not been encouraging'. My imagination leads me down a corridor of dark possibilities in which you accidentally poisoned the vicar with a jar of rancid courgette preserve and then panicked and covered your tracks by burying him in the churchyard. But I expect what really happened is more mundane and that your produce generated little to no interest. How dispiriting to make a huge batch, only to sell one pot of the damned stuff to a well-wishing friend and have to push the rest down the waste disposal.

In any case, this tendency to give up quickly leaves me wondering whether you are not keener on cloaking yourself in the identity of an entrepreneur than you are on the tough reality of actually being one. That is not a judgement. This is a surprisingly common form of self-delusion. In fact, I have an identical attitude towards being a triathlete.

To conclude, my advice is that, whatever you think of doing by way of a business, within reason, just get on with it. You won't really learn anything until you dive in and find out what you are capable of. Hopefully this will have lifted your morale and made you excited for the future and what it has in store for you and Katya. Regards to you both and good luck.

Dear Jack, I cannot stand my mother-in-law. She is a bully to me and a control freak and nothing I ever do is ever good enough, but my husband, who is her only son, is in her thrall. What is the best way to show her in her true colours when she next visits?

Rachel (not my real name), King's Lynn

Hello 'Rachel'. The issue of in-laws is a common feature of agony columns, sitcoms and murder trials all over the world. Many who choose the path of marriage remember well that special moment of solemn promises and sacred vows that bind them for eternity to their chosen life partner, even if they do, forever after, ponder the injustice that this should involve having to be nice to two old people they couldn't care less about.

Of course, although the principle of commitment remains largely unchanged, over the years the wording has altered to suit modern sensibilities. Understandably the pledge to obey is seen by many as anachronistic and inappropriate in this day and age and has, in pretty much every case, been replaced with constant marital rowing. It was certainly the case in my marriage until, a few years in after a long and emotional conversation with Jane, she decided that despite obeisance being absent in our original vows, it would be best if I just did what I was told to do. And so it has been ever since. Thus ended a power struggle that I sometimes compare with that seen between humans and Labradors.

But my reason for raising the topic of the actual marriage ceremony is this: to whom do we make our vows? Is it solely to our intended, or are these pledges also being made to various members of their extended family? When you repeated the celebrant's invocations to love and to cherish, were you addressing your soon-to-be husband or were you also swearing affection to his mother? I think you know the answer. His were the eyes you looked into when you spoke, not hers. She has not yet earned your love or anything like it. She doubtless spent the ceremony glaring at the back of your head like a gargoyle and wishing you had tripped over your veil on your way up the aisle, split your head open on the end of a pew and done everyone a favour.

> **As everyone knows, apart from toddlers, there are two types of people who can utterly ruin a wedding – relatives and friends**

And the less said about the reception the better. As everyone knows, apart from toddlers, there are two types of people who can utterly ruin a wedding – relatives and friends. Toddlers at least have an excuse. For instance, as a small child, how was I to know that my older cousins were in fact lying to me when they insisted that the uncut five-tier cake was 'a bit like a bouncy castle and you can jump on it if you want'? Naturally I did want; I slipped my shoes off and dived in. One doesn't think of a marquee as having an echo – maybe my memory is playing tricks on me – but I can still hear the bride's reverberating scream: 'Get that f***ing little f***er out of here.' The older cousins were more than ready to oblige.

Now, about your husband. Let's say his name is Neil. It isn't Neil's fault that he is his overbearing mother's only son and is caught in the pincers created when filial loyalty and romantic love find themselves hinged together. Some psychotherapists might encourage you to applaud him just for loving his mum. But, as qualities go, that is hardly a ringing endorsement. It simply puts him in the same category as Hitler, Norman Bates and eighties pop sensation Bros. Others might say that Neil should stop inviting his mother over, refuse to answer her calls and play for time until she can finally, thank God, be put into a local nursing home and, to all intents and purposes, forgotten about.

My experience suggests that neither of these scenarios provides a satisfactory solution to your particular problem. I have already explained why the first is unsuitable and the second option won't do as nursing homes can be pricey, long-term, and without wanting to sound cold and cynical, you'd be better not to chip away too much at the old inheritance.

And so a third option arises that I believe will help you to push back against this bullying figure in your life. Shun her. Subtly, elegantly, without fanfare or fuss, but most definitely: shun her. Little things will do it. You will see how they add up to the equivalent of a mighty assault but without the evidence. When she comes to stay over, this time don't make the bed up for her. Put the sheets out and let her do it. Don't keep a supply of her favourite tea. She doesn't really like Earl Grey anyway, it's just an affectation. Perhaps when she asks you a question like, 'Don't you think Neil would love it if the kitchen was nice and tidy when he gets in?', snort with laughter. Then, when she turns to stare at you with those mannequin eyes, be sure to be looking at your phone and say, 'Oh sorry, just a text from a friend asking after you.' Next time she cooks for you and Neil, leave out the usual compliments that you dutifully pay her and don't ask for the recipe. Follow that up by taking one mouthful of the dessert and then rushing to the lavatory. Sound concerned about the fact that she still drives. Buy her one of those tartan shopping trollies as a present and suggest it might be best for everyone if she thought about selling the car. What you will notice is a gradual attrition of her status as sure as the highest rock face is slowly massaged into sand by the soft but unceasing fingers of the tide. You will see how the balance of power changes and how she becomes the one who is lacking confidence and needy of your approval.

Learn the fine art of making someone in your life feel unwelcome and inept. It is a skill that will both solve your current problem and prove to be invaluable when your son gets married.

> I can't stop thinking about cross-dressing but I feel certain my girlfriend will think I've lost it if I broach the subject with her. I don't want it to be a secret but I'm worried about scaring her off. What do you think?
>
> (Via SMS)

Give it a go and if she makes a fuss tell her not to get your knickers in a twist.

Dear Jack, How do I get off the couch?

Julia, Australia (via Twitter)

Thank you for your question, Julia. I am going to assume that you are referring to a lack of motivation on your part that has led to a state of lethargy. If I am wrong and you have genuinely discovered that for some bizarre reason you can no longer stand up, then you need urgent assistance. Hopefully you have a phone within reach and can call the emergency services or a neighbour.

I note that your location is somewhere in Australia and that causes me to worry that you have no neighbours within a fortnight's drive and that you could very well be stuck on a couch in a tin-roofed bungalow with nothing but sheep, tumbleweed and the occasional kangaroo skeleton for miles and miles. If that is the case, then I freely admit that I cannot help. By the time this book gets published it's very possible that you still won't have been discovered unless you have one of those sheepdogs like Lassie that goes to get help if you're trapped down a well – which for the sake of this response, you might as well be. In fact it would be better if you were because, as improbable as it is that a dog would ever really be taken seriously when trying to explain its owner's dire predicament via the limited language of barking, the idea that a couple of pissed-up old bushwhackers would do anything other than order another cold beer because you can't get up is beyond credibility. Allow me to set the scene for you using my skill as a screenwriter:

SCENE: *A typical bar in outback Australia. Two dirty old blokes are at the bar drinking beer. One of them lazily gets up and puts a coin in the jukebox. He hits a button and some didgeridoo music starts. A sheepdog enters and barks once.*

FIRST BUSHWHACKER

Struth, Micky, isn't that Julia's dog?

MICKY

What, Julia from Bleak Valley sheep station?

FIRST BUSHWHACKER

Yeah, that Julia.

MICKY

Blimey, First Bushwhacker, I think you're right.

DOG

Woof.

MICKY

Here, I think he's trying to tell us something. (*To the dog*) What's that you say, mate?

DOG

Woof. Woof, woof.

MICKY

Julia can't get off the couch?

DOG

Woof.

At this point First Bushwhacker ushers the sheepdog out of the bar and returns to sit down with his beer. He turns to Micky.

FIRST BUSHWHACKER

Bloody dog.

MICKY

Yeah. And bloody Julia.

FIRST BUSHWACKER

Yeah. She can get *herself* off the bloody couch.

MICKY

Yeah. Bloody right.

END

Obviously that's just off the top of my head. I could write it up to a full-length screenplay should the interest be there. My thought is that the sheepdog then goes to get help at the post office etc. There is a darker version in which you are eventually discovered in a very bad way having had to resort to eating a cushion.*

By now you may be thinking, 'Jack, that's all very well but the part of Australia that I live in is metropolitan, contemporary

---

* Perhaps here is as good a time and place as any to finally quash the unkind rumour that my last screenplay was rejected by every single UK-based broadcaster and studio on the grounds of its 'crass stereotyping and infantile nature'. This is simply not the case. That quote was taken out of context and was included in one single letter from the BBC Drama Department, which went on to say in a very friendly, my-door-is-always-open-to-you way (and this is the bit that always gets left out) 'Yours *sincerely*, Jane Treadway, Head of Scripted Drama'. She didn't need to say that. Nice touch.

and vibrant – even if I can't be arsed to get off the couch to go out and enjoy it.'

Fair point, Julia. And I'd like to state here and now that I never generalise or resort to lazy clichés. So let's go back to the problem and not agonise over the precise location.

As I see it, you have become depressed and isolated and this has led to your inertia. 'Couches', as you call them, are very popular in Australia and almost every house has at least four. The trouble is that they are comfortable and it is surprisingly easy to spend days and days doing nothing but lying around watching daytime TV with the occasional snooze in between episodes of *Neighbours* and news bulletins telling you to evacuate your home because of bush fires.

So my advice to you is to aim at increasing your activity bit by bit on a daily basis. There are apps available that can be of great help in this. Many people recommend one called Couch to 5k but beware of unhelpful imitations. Couch to Fridge proved a disastrous download in my case. After only two weeks I had put on a significant amount of weight and eventually had to call an ambulance to help me as I was so unhealthy I couldn't even change channels on the TV. (In the event, it transpired that the batteries in the remote had gone dead. An easy mistake to make.

> **Many people recommend one called Couch to 5k but beware of unhelpful imitations. Couch to Fridge proved a disastrous download in my case**

Not that you would think so from the undisguised contempt of the paramedics. I still maintain: if you're going to call someone a time-wasting twat, at least say it to their face. Don't just mutter it to each other as you make your way back to your oh-so-important ambulance.)

So good luck, Julia. Take small steps towards a more active life, one day at a time. And remember, you are not alone, even in the middle of Australia. The internet is a wonderful tool for staying connected with those we love as well as essential services. Hopefully you do have broadband, or at the very least an old car tyre you can set alight to attract attention from a passing aeroplane. I hope that this has helped and encouraged you to try harder, knowing that the consequences of not doing so really are grim. Nobody I know has ever eaten a cushion and said it was a good experience.

> *Since lockdown, my husband Steve has been permanently working from home and it is driving me crazy. He treats the whole house like his office, shouting at his computer on Zoom calls, and if he asks me what we're having for lunch one more time, I think I might walk out. I just want him to go back to the office so I can have the house to myself. Should I say something to him?*
>
> *Michelle, Wigan*

Well, Michelle, you can't imagine how many letters I get on this subject. It's as if Covid was not content with its initial deathly strike but had to impose on us an endless succession of horrors, not least of which is the work from home (WFH) craze that so many of us now find ourselves blighted with. You don't say whether you are currently working, but if you are, I'm going to guess that you too work from home (otherwise the problem would not have arisen) and that you have quietly and efficiently designed your life in the most pragmatic way you could, enabling all the different elements of your world to coexist in harmony. I'm picturing you, maybe, with a laptop on the kitchen table, making phone calls and filling out spreadsheets but also occasionally stretching across to the washing machine and switching it to a final spin, emailing clients while clicking away on Tesco Direct and so on.

Enter Steve.

Please do not feel guilty about the negativity that you feel towards your husband's new work arrangement. In marriage we vow to love each other under all manner of diverse conditions: for better, for worse, for richer, for poorer, in sickness and in health. If you had written to me saying you're fed up with your husband because he makes less money than you thought he would, then I would ask you to look at your values and examine how far you have strayed from the person you were when you fell in love with Steve. If you had said you're fed up with your husband because he is ill and you hate looking after him, then I would really want you to reassess what kind of person you have become and how you can find a way back to the humanity that you have abandoned. However, neither of these clauses is the issue. The marriage vow that we are clearly discussing here is 'for better, for worse'. The plain truth of it is that your husband has become worse than he was at being an acceptable person to live with and I don't care what any vicar, priest or frumpy registrar has to say about it, you cannot be expected to deal with that as if it isn't happening.

Furthermore, although not actually a theologian, I feel I can say with some authority that this is not even what God expects of you. Look how he dealt with Adam and Eve: the one thing he asked of them was not to eat from that particular apple tree – other than that, the place is yours to enjoy, he said. And it's paradise; they've got waterfalls, sunshine, probably some early form of Deliveroo – basically everything they could want. They don't even need to wear clothes – just enjoy themselves, but stay off the prize apples. And what do they do? They eat one of the prize apples because – well, that's it, nobody really knows. Maybe it was the snake, maybe they got bored. Maybe they were just a bit thick and forgot. Whatever it was, the reason for raising this is that God was having no truck with it and booted them out. No second chances. My point is that if God doesn't tolerate bad behaviour, then why should any of us? And as vows go, 'for better, for worse' is a non-starter in my book.

Marriage is a contract, but no lawyer would seriously let you enter into a contract as ambiguous and open to abuse as that. You wouldn't sign a contract with some bum-crack builder that says you are going to pay him, regardless of whether he does the job well or not, would you? No, of course you wouldn't. Why would you pay cash upfront for a kitchen extension to someone who doesn't know how to stop his own trousers falling down? So the time has come to overturn the deal you made with Steve and renegotiate.

I mentioned earlier that WFH is a horror and you, more than most, understand why. But there are some readers who might not have had the (dubious) benefit of your experience, Michelle, so it is worth me taking a moment to help put them in the picture.

In London, a couple of years ago, there was a spate of complaints in the press and social media about men sitting on the Tube with their legs agape, as if they owned the train. This was labelled 'man-spreading' and became quite the talking point for several months among newspaper columnists who decided they hated this proprietorial posturing and had nothing better to write about at the time.

So, Steve is 'man-spreading'. He is being a bit of an oaf and this is made more acutely offensive because he is doing it in the very personal space of your home. What makes this a particularly flammable situation is that your home is, by definition, a shared space, and that means that Steve's failure to acknowledge this is starting to feel like a denial of you and your right to be there on equal terms.

I will return us to that Tube carriage to illuminate further your situation. We have all shared a journey with the guy who makes those loud, self-important phone calls. There is something especially trying about only being able to eavesdrop on one half of a conversation and certainly there is no entertainment in it. I imagine you have this experience for much of the day, every day. Whatever you are doing in the house has to be done to the drone of Steve banging on about sales figures, forecasts and projections with his regional manager. Zoom has much to answer for, not least those squelchy conference-call voices coming from the spare room, or 'office' as Steve now calls it. Your home has become a babel of nonsense jargon, as if *Line of Duty* was playing endlessly in the background. Michelle, you deserve better.

> **Your home has become a babel of nonsense jargon, as if *Line of Duty* was playing endlessly in the background**

All this is easily serious enough to have you screaming into a cushion and wondering how long it will be before you snap and take a hammer to his laptop. But then you have the added injustice of being expected to cater. Just when you think it's gone quiet and you might calm down and make a cup of coffee for yourself, you turn round and there's bloody Steve asking what's for lunch. It won't be long before he accidentally calls you 'Subway' or asks you to stamp his loyalty card when you make him a sandwich.

The thing is, Michelle, that Steve (and I'm only trying to be fair here, as always) is almost certainly unaware that he is making your life a living hell. All he can think is that he doesn't have to travel anywhere and that he's some sort of pioneer in this awful global shift towards working from home. He probably even tells himself that the two of you have more quality time and doesn't get it that you were happier pre-Covid when you hardly ever saw him and if you really missed him you had his Y-fronts hanging on the radiator as a comfort.

There is a limit to how much time any couple should spend together; that is not a reflection on the nature of relationships – it is a pure fact that accounts for the widespread existence of commuting. It is as if we have known all along that the togetherness versus separation ratio is crucial and one that we neglect at the cost of our mental health. One of the immediate and inevitable consequences of the Covid-19 crisis is that we were forced to abandon that understanding of ourselves. Perhaps a sensible way forward would be for all those now-disused offices to be reconfigured into comfortable proxy homes where people can go every day because their partners have taken over their actual home and filled it with flip charts.

Until that happens, you need a solution so that life becomes bearable and you don't write to me again asking if I know a good lawyer who can get you off the charge of pushing your husband down the stairs. Or, worse still, I hear from someone called Steve asking for the name of a good proctologist who can repair the damage done to him by his wife who became inexplicably aggressive with a baguette one day when he asked her what was for lunch.

I would suggest taking yourself to the local library, but of course they too are closed due to coronavirus, leaving some members with no option but to tear random pages out of their own books. A lot of coffee shops are still only doing takeaways, but I am sure they will soon be full once again with pasty-faced customers nursing a flat white all day just to use their internet.

However, maybe you have a garden shed that you could convert into a studio/hermitage for yourself. It's unfair that there seems to be no such thing as a 'woman-cave'. A man-cave is typically like a railway signal box with craft ale and a vinyl collection. In design terms it's like a fusion of the three blokes everyone avoids in the pub. But your shed could be a sophisticated take on the garden room with comfortable furniture to make work more pleasant, but then also a chaise longue or even a bed, a small fridge for tonic waters and gin, music of your choice playing in the background, a childproof cabinet for your Xanax, a duvet and an eye-mask.

Set yourself up like this and you can drift through the next few months, or even years, anaesthetised from the relentlessly negative presence of your husband. It worked for my wife and it can work for you. Good luck, Michelle.

My husband has taken up cooking, having never shown any interest before. He now thinks he's Gordon Ramsay (and sounds like him when things aren't going to plan) despite the fact that what he serves up is pretty much inedible – last night it was chicken that was still raw in the middle with rice that you needed to cut with a knife and fork. He doesn't take criticism well but keeps getting in the kitchen before I can. What should I do?

First of all, I suggest you buy a swear box and a sick bucket. With the money that you make, enrol your husband in a cooking course as a surprise. Let the teacher do all the heavy lifting of putting him straight and hopefully he will come home with a more realistic opinion of his achievements to date, which can best be summed up as attempted manslaughter. If he still doesn't learn, announce that you had better prepare your own food from now on as you have started a very strict low-gluten, no-carb, salmonella-free diet for medical reasons.

Dear Jack, for a long time now I have had an uneasy sense that my life doesn't match the expectations I had for it and often it feels like everyone else is having a better time and doing everything better than I am. I am 28 and although I have a reasonable job and am in a relationship, I have a permanent feeling of being disappointed and cannot put my finger on why this should be. I can't talk about it to my girlfriend as she will panic and think it is her fault. My mates tell me to stop moaning and my parents have always been unable to talk about emotions etc. I would so like to be able to cheer up and appreciate how lucky I am. What should I do?

(Name and location withheld)

Thank you for your email. To start with I would like to address you by name but fully respect your wishes. I hope, therefore, that you won't object to me calling you Glen in my reply to you. If you don't like it, then I guess you'll just add it to your long list of disappointments and I apologise for instantly making things worse rather than better. Either way, Glen, I hope that you read on and that we are able to make some sense of what you're going through.

From where I'm looking, my assessment is that your problem is twofold: namely, you feel generally disillusioned and you have no one that you can talk to about these feelings. A bit like going to Centre Parcs on your own.

So, I'll deal with these two elements in reverse order. First of all, you have no one to talk to. When you say that your mates tell you to stop moaning, it is worth considering the context in which you have raised your issues in the past. If it's a gloriously warm Sunday lunchtime in a nice pub garden and you're all enjoying a pint and packet of pork scratchings, chatting about the football or last night's TV or whatever, that would be a bad time to chip in with a statement like 'No, but seriously guys, don't you ever think about how pointless and shit life is?' I can see that being received as something of a session wrecker. Your friends could be forgiven for their lack of reply and sideways glances to one another. Maybe it's not the first time you've bombed the small talk with your doom and those sideways glances are evolving into wearisome raised eyebrows as your friends silently realise that yet another pleasant afternoon is being ruined by gloomy Glen. I don't for one moment intend to belittle how you are feeling, but it is important that you get some perspective on how others might see your company.

Your girlfriend, on the other hand, might be more sympathetic. I understand your concern that she will not cope well with discovering how you feel. However, it seems you haven't actually tried to speak to her. You have assumed that her reaction would be to blame herself. Perhaps put it to the test, try her out as a sounding board with a less daunting problem. Maybe say how frustrating it is that your parents never want to listen if you have something important to say. Your girlfriend might pick up on this and ask what you would like to discuss with them. Again, as with your mates, don't then just chirp up with, 'Oh, you know, just how rubbish my life is.' Who wouldn't be upset to hear that from the person they are in a long-term relationship with? It would be very hard not to take that as a direct criticism of oneself. Luckily, my wife only ever says it to me as a joke and then, for comic effect, insists it's not a joke, which is even funnier.

So, start on a gentler trajectory like, 'I'd like to be able to talk to them about how my job is going and how I feel about it.' Much less challenging, don't you agree? Hopefully, she will respond warmly to your new confidential tone and invite you to talk about your work. Of course, it could be that she is entirely inappropriate for this type of conversation. Some people can't help their knee-jerk response to anything that smacks remotely of emotion. If it becomes clear she is the wrong person for the job ('Oh give it a rest, you big girl's blouse. I can't stand all that touchy-feely claptrap. I'm not Oprah bloody Winfrey. Sort yourself out or clear the fuck off, you big twat'), then you will have learnt a valuable lesson relating to your girlfriend's suitability as a listener. Or member of the human race. Anyway, hopefully that won't be the case and she'll come through for you.

> **Luckily, my wife only ever says it to me as a joke and then, for comic effect, insists it's not a joke, which is even funnier**

Your parents can have a free pass on this, I think. Surely they've done enough for you by now and don't deserve to have their retirement ruined by old sourpuss Glen coming round with his smacked-arse expression and bad news. Besides, by my calculations they were probably teenagers in the seventies which means, if they're anything like me, they will still be struggling to come to terms with the fact that they knowingly wore flares and owned a Brotherhood of Man LP. That's enough shame and guilt to last a lifetime; they don't need to be burdened by your angst as well.

Now, Glen, let us look at the forces in play that are making you reflect with such negativity upon your life. By understanding the source of your malaise you can control and even remedy it. My take on things is that you are too concerned, possibly even preoccupied, with how everyone around you is faring. This can be unhealthy as you inevitably end up comparing how others appear with how you feel – a common mistake but one that has a corrosive effect on our sense of well-being, success, attractiveness etc.

One area that we should consider is that of social media. Nowadays it's hard to imagine that there was a time when people would confine their gossip, loves, emotions, what they had for breakfast, lunch, dinner and so on to a small trusted coterie of friends and family. But today, all that has changed thanks to Facebook, Instagram, Twitter and all the various platforms on which we parade our lives. Generally, people use social media for one of two reasons, namely, to show off or sound off. While it would be hard to overstate the pervasive effect of social media on every aspect of our lives, it has a particular influence on our sense of self. I would liken its impact on us all to that of the background music they play in some supermarkets. The tempo and pitch is carefully calibrated to prevent us from detecting it but at the same time to numb our senses into a trance of inexplicable despair. It's very similar to that feeling we have the first time we hear a medley of Beatles hits played by an orchestra. So it is with social media, the easy-listening music of our time – apparently harmless but actually a form of evil.

My belief is that your worldview has been formed by a constant stream of blogs, vlogs and tweets. Bombarded with a relentless storm of content offering peeks into carefully styled and air-brushed lifestyles, it is little wonder that you find yourself with a gnawing sense of underachievement.

But social media can't be blamed entirely for the lifestyle pressures that we all find ourselves under and which are, in my judgement, causing you feelings of depression. Print should not go unmentioned in the conversation about subliminal influence. Glossy magazines in particular ply us with a non-stop stream of pictorials. Who hasn't, while waiting for the dentist, flicked through a magazine featuring beautiful people showing off their immaculate homes? A typical piece from one I saw recently read: 'Driving through the West Country during a weekend break from London, jewellery designer Poo Flusher and City broker husband Sholto chanced upon the dilapidated seventeenth-century pigsty on a four-acre plot with a "for sale" sign. After a phone call to the agent and a nervous ten-minute wait, it was theirs. Architect friend Hans Von Rotringpen was called upon to draw up plans for the ten-bedroom contemporary house made of industrial-grade concrete and polished steel that now prominently graces the Somerset landscape. "We wanted more land so that the children could have kangaroos, a pet bison, a Gypsy caravan with real Gypsies and a nine-acre Go Ape-style play area," explains Poo, "and luckily, just as the house was completed our neighbours suddenly said they were moving, so we bought their farm as well, which has a fantastic barn for parties." With the help of Los Angeles-based interior designer Dougray Mostly, the stunning new-build was ready to become a home. Dougray's cleverly chosen Borrow & Foul off-white shades of bat's breath, granny hair and old hanky are brought together by Sholto's extensive collection of ethnic art acquired over the years on his travels . . .'

To feature in *Hello!* magazine you have to be reasonably well known and fairly rich,* as well as happy to be photographed in every room of your house wearing (this is never explained) a different outfit in each picture. The less well known and rich are handled by the equally gaudy and exclamatory *OK!* You can take your pick. Do you want to see a minor royal with his golden Labrador in a rococo drawing room or a soap

> **We wanted more land so that the children could have kangaroos, a pet bison, a Gypsy caravan with real Gypsies and a nine-acre Go Ape-style play area**

star boxercising in a lean-to conservatory? Well, between them, *Hello!* and *OK!* have it covered. Possibly it's just a bit of harmless

---

* Although very occasionally a humble-pie edition will feature someone on their uppers, which gives the subject the chance to put a positive sheen onto an obviously less than ideal turn of fortune: 'Actor Michael M. Jones (*The Bill*, *Casualty*, *Big Brother*) on how bankruptcy and his time in prison for shoplifting are the best things that ever happened to him . . .'

titillation to spy on public figures in this way. But my suggestion is that it is increasingly easy to flood our lives with this content without realising its impact on our psychological well-being.

Or, look at it this way. Most of us can surely relate to having a friend that we don't really like. And we find that we don't really like them because every time we meet them we come away feeling diminished in some way. The 'friend', in nearly all cases, makes you feel this way through bragging and oneupmanship. This rarely presents in crude form. Boasting is like flatulence: somehow, the more subtle it is, the more offensive the whiff. 'Friends' like these must be avoided as much as possible because what they do is to treat you as if you are some kind of ego-ladder. They climb on top of you, each step being another casually mentioned achievement, one more incidental achievement slipped into the chat. So, naturally, encounters with such people leave you feeling pushed down and reduced in stature.

The type of media that I have mentioned above can do the same thing, Glen. My suggestion to you is you take a sabbatical from it all in order to experience what your life is like when it is not forced to bow to the entirely manufactured representation of other people's lives that can engulf us if we don't learn to just look away from it.

Of course I could be wrong. It might be that you're just a rotten, miserable little drip who can't stop griping, in which case there is little more I can do except remind you of my motto: 'Wherever you go, spread a little happiness and before you know it, you'll be happy too.' It works for me and it can work for you too, Glen.

Hi Jack. I have just discovered that my wife's brother, John, is coming for Christmas with his wife Miya and two children. The children are fine as they are the same age as ours and get along. The problem is the adults. John is incredibly opinionated and starts arguments on any subject at the drop of a hat. This is not helped by the fact that he is a conspiracy theorist who genuinely believes all kinds of strange things relating to everything from the moon landing to Covid. At times it can be unbearable to listen to him spouting his nonsense. My wife (Lise) always briefs me before they arrive, reminding me to change the subject if things get heated etc. But I really can't stay quiet when someone is making ridiculous statements at the end of the dining table. It's different for Lise because she grew up with John and can deal with him more easily and Miya is a really nice person but she is Japanese and her English has never been strong so she either doesn't really understand or is pretending not to. I find myself dreading seeing them. Please can you help me with a plan or at least some coping strategies.

> *Phil, Worcester (PS. All the names have been changed)*

Hi Phil. Reading your email made me envy Miya. What a gift, to be able to legitimately not engage in conversation with stupid people and never cause offence. She has cracked this one, although not in a way that can help you unless you feign a road accident and pretend the head trauma has meant that, while you can still enjoy wine and food, you are no longer capable of understanding or speaking English. Personally, that is pretty much how I end up at Christmas anyway so can testify that if you make good use of the festive provisions, your performance should come naturally.

It is important to stress that putting on a show like this over Christmas would require your entire family's full support. Acting out an acute disorder is undoubtedly an effective way of manipulating people and situations to suit your needs but it can rebound disastrously if your deception is exposed. Let us say you've gone to all the trouble of bandaging your head and appearing in your pyjamas to give the appearance of someone convalescing. Lise has primed her brother and sister-in-law not to be too shocked by your appearance and told them that since the crash you are, what they call in medical circles, *whickerus maximus*, or 'basket case' and can only communicate through basic mime and the use of a jotter. You have very realistically failed to recognise John and Miya and slowly written on your notepad for them: 'Hello. My name is Philip. What is your names? (*sic*)' followed by 'happy easter'. So far, it seems to be working. Miya has nodded appreciatively and John has already decided to keep things light and certainly to avoid introducing his latest bizarre theory, which is that BBC Two's *Springwatch* has been hacked by foreign players (naturally, led by Chris Packham) and could be deployed to spread TB at any time.

All is going to plan until your children come running in. Instantly, you realise that like the criminal in a Poirot story, you made one fatal error. You did not tell the kids what you were doing. After less than a minute watching you struggle with your Biro and pad to explain that you would like another drink, they tactlessly blurt out, 'What's wrong with Dad? Is it a game? Can we play?' And before you can say Munchausen (or write it, for that matter), your cover is blown and you have some explaining to do. With no backup story, Christmas is a glum affair of stilted chatter and mumbled excuses that hardly begin to explain your appalling behaviour. Your claim that you were just doing it for a laugh is not one that was ever going to land well with somebody as logically stupid as John and is only met with the po-faced but not unreasonable question, 'What's funny about brain injury?'

Speaking of laughs, a more straightforward tactic would be to treat anything and everything that John says as if he meant it as a joke. This probably won't even be hard given the nature of what conspiracists come up with. The difficult part will just be keeping up the laughter as he reels off his endless list of absurd notions. The trick is not to start too big so that you always have plenty left in the mirth tank for when he gets really ridiculous. For instance, let us imagine the following scene. You're having a drink and 'White Christmas' is playing in the background. Instead of any number of innocuous comments he could make, John characteristically goes for, 'You know Bing Crosby was hit by the CIA, don't you? They shot him with a poison dart when he was playing golf.' Instead of taking the bait and expressing astonishment, just chuckle at the idea, maybe throwing in something like, 'Of course he was. That idiot had it coming, wearing knitwear like that.' If you do this effectively, the laughter alone will be sufficiently derisive for John to think twice about what he says next. However, don't bank on it. Such individuals are notoriously thick-skinned and are easily capable of misinterpreting laughter as an indication of interest, even respect, rather than the humiliation that it should rightly signal.

> **Such individuals are notoriously thick-skinned and are easily capable of misinterpreting laughter as an indication of interest**

Do not be discouraged if results are not apparent at this early stage. You have all of Christmas to work your magic and should proceed with confidence, knowing that at any time, you can step the ribaldry up a notch whenever it is necessary. Already you will be feeling better because you have found a way of not having to let your guest go unpunished every time he opens his mouth with another daft utterance. You have liberated yourself from the slog of futile debate and can now enjoy having the upper hand.

Remember, the very last thing you should do is lock horns with John. This would result in what I describe as an asymmetrical exchange. What this means, basically, is that John will put forward an easily refutable, demonstrably false theory but your factual and verifiable counterpoint will not be recognised as legitimate because, according to John, you either won't 'open your eyes and see what's going on, man' or because you are in on it too. Therefore, never loosen your grip during their stay. Deliberately misinterpret everything he says as a joke, so that he begins to feel that his position is going to require significant effort to uphold.

Defending his views from brazen, outright laughter will be a far less comfortable matter for him because people like John crave being taken seriously. One of the key functions of a conspiracy theory is that it allows its proponents a false sense of intellectualism. The language of academia is as good a vector of rubbish as it is of sound ideas, without requiring the speaker to discern between the two. When your brother-in-law asserts that the pyramids were built by visiting aliens, you can be certain that he will support this with lists of corroborating 'evidence'. Please resist the natural impulse to challenge him on this, knowing that your new weapon, ridicule, will do in a moment what hours of heated argument will never achieve. Celebrate John as a cone-hatted dunce rather than revere him as the profound thinker and sage that he wants you to believe he is. Soon you will be relishing every word that parps from his mouth, knowing it to be potential comedy gold. Think of the fun you can have. No more head-scratching as you become increasingly disorientated by his insane gibberish; now you can turn it to your advantage by repeating his words for comic effect – 'Hear that, kids? Uncle John says coronavirus comes from 5G. Everyone stay clear of phone masts . . . ha ha ha.' Then sit back and let the children do the rest with their gift for honesty. 'You're funny,' they'll say joyfully. 'Was that in your cracker?' and 'You're a silly man,' pointing at him. Hopefully one of the littlest hecklers will get carried away and flick a mince pie at him, hitting him in the eye to complete the denouncement.

You, on the other hand, will be beyond reproach of course, merely the innocent conveyor of John's joke. The children's laughter will reverberate uncontrollably as John picks pieces of pastry from his hair. Now is the time for the knockout blow as you continue with, 'It's like when he said the moon landing was staged in a TV studio . . .' Lise will nudge you to stop but find it irresistibly funny as her eyes fill with tears of laughter and the children shriek hysterically despite not having a clue what it means. Even Miya will join in, abandoning her pretence of not understanding and raucously remind you all of how John had claimed that the giveaway was the reflection in Neil Armstrong's visor that clearly showed a full camera crew if looked at a certain way. Cue Coca-Cola and Christmas wine being spat out in uncontrolled hysteria round the table.

Using this method of turning John's own wife and children against him with your jeering mirth, I firmly contend that this Christmas will be your happiest ever. If things go really well it could even cause John to give fresh thought to why he constantly interprets bad news as evidence of foul play. Of course, sometimes life's most complex challenges are best understood through the lens of fantasy, but that is why we have art. And Ativan, for that matter. The conspiracist, however, does something quite different, applying fiction to that which can ultimately be explained either as wickedness, coincidence or misfortune – concepts that are simple to grasp but often too painful to accept. I hope that you find something useful in my reply and that your Christmas is consequently more enjoyable than you were predicting for you and your family.

Dear Jack, after ten years of marriage is it too late to ask my wife to stop leaving the door open when she goes to the loo?

(Via SMS)

I know only too well that feeling of lazily putting up with something for years and then suddenly realising that it is totally unacceptable and ruining your day. In my case, I stopped watching *Good Morning Britain* and things started to improve. But we can't avoid everything we don't like seeing so easily. So I suggest you tell your kids you'll buy them ice cream if they pretend to cry when they see their mum on the lavatory. If you don't have kids, train the dog to howl and play dead. If you don't have a dog, kick the cat flap and ask her why the cat just ran out of the house, terrified. If you don't have kids or pets, stand in the doorway talking to her about your favourite pizza topping while handing her pieces of toilet roll. Pretty quickly, she'll start to see wee time as me time and lock the door.

> *Dear Jack. My golden retriever bitch can't resist humping the corduroy trouser-clad leg of a male friend. Can you suggest a way round this embarrassment?*
>
> *(Via SMS)*

There's an obvious solution to this one. As this has happened more than once it's clear that your friend is a pervert and knowingly comes round wearing corduroys to provoke your dog into sexual activity. Dump him and find new friends.

I'm pregnant and my best friend has just had a baby. A couple of months ago, I told her that I wanted to call my daughter Sadie and at that point she hadn't decided on any names. Yesterday, I received the text from her telling me that she's just named her newborn daughter Sadie! I can't believe it. It's not even a particularly common name. I know it seems like a small thing, but I feel incredibly hurt. Is there anything I can do?

(Via SMS)

This is a classic case of imposter syndrome. Unfortunately she won't stop at baby names as she's clearly a right nutcase. Tell her you are moving and show her the details of a house you hope to buy that's hundreds of miles away. In all likelihood she'll go behind your back and buy it, you'll never need to see her again and can call your daughter whatever you want.

> *My boyfriend and I have been together for more than five years now. We have a great relationship and after saving carefully for the last three years, we've been able to put a deposit on a small house. I really want to have children but my boyfriend is very unsure as he thinks it will spoil everything that we have worked so hard for. What should I do?*
>
> *Lynn, Bedfordshire*

Well, Lynn, it is hard to reply without saying up front that I totally agree with your boyfriend. He is absolutely right, having children will wreck everything. That is what they do and it's OK to say it because you can love your kids while hating what they do to your life. This is the great dichotomy that defines parenthood. It also means that I am able to agree with your boyfriend *and* support your ambition to start a family.

Way too many people mindlessly drift into having children without any understanding of the repercussions it will inevitably have on their lifestyle, finances, relationship, recreational activities, physical and mental health, spiritual well-being, car, everything. It is important and healthy to recognise these facts, partly because, in so doing, you mitigate their effect. I believe this is what your boyfriend is subconsciously doing. Even though he thinks he does not want and therefore will not have children, his biological nerve centre disagrees and will see to it that he does. Somewhere in that mysterious grey mush of chemical interactions that is his brain, neurons are conspiring to ensure that his impulse to reproduce will triumph. They even create a smokescreen of inner dissent so that the man perkily believes he is being logical and sensible in his resolve not to sire – even environmentally responsible. All to no avail, however, as his libido will of course wipe such pretences away like a stormy tide obliterating a row of sand castles.

Enjoy your partner's protestations, Lynn. When he explains that he doesn't want anything or anyone to come between the two of you, tell him how adorable that is. When he says life is perfect as it is, agree winsomely, safe in the knowledge that, really, he has no say in the matter anyway. But also pay heed to his scepticism. As I have said, it can help mitigate some of the downsides of having children.

This last point could hardly be more important because, without scepticism, one of two unfortunate tendencies will emerge. The first is depression. Sometimes this is brought on by the simple anticlimax that can occur when, after all that waiting and excitement and preparation, you find yourself shattered with exhaustion, traumatised by the actual birth and not as smitten with the baby as you imagined you would be. A bit like when you get a new Apple product.

The second is euphoria. This is almost as bad because it means that, although the new parents are ecstatic, they lose all sense of perspective and take umbrage at anyone who doesn't share their joy at every gurgle, chuckle, scream and bowel movement of their tiny tot with equal rapture. In some ways, postnatal euphoria is worse than postnatal depression because nobody seeks medical help for being too happy. Yet, for all our sakes, they really should.

Scepticism is like a philosophical Dyno-Rod, prodding and poking at those troublesome mental blockages that cause you to overflow with soppy emotions

So scepticism is good; it is a life-saver. Scepticism is the sanitary system of your mind. It purges you of all the unhelpful crap that accumulates in your thought processes. Scepticism is like a philosophical Dyno-Rod, prodding and poking at those troublesome mental blockages that cause you to overflow with soppy emotions.

This all adds up to you being in a good position. Be patient, appreciate your partner's reluctance as a positive and, last but not least, place more trust in the primal commands of biology and I suspect you will have everything you want. Good luck, Lynn.

Hi Sean, I'm sorry you feel that way and that you thought it an acceptable idea to use my new book to have a go at me in this very personal tone. I don't think that either of us really wants to wash our dirty linen in public but since you launched the first salvo, I will respond in kind.

It is true that I have been preoccupied with various things recently. Unlike you, I still have a career; two in fact, if you include my new and successful psychotherapy sideline – hence this much-demanded book. Yes, this has meant that, at times, I have not been able to muster the energy to communicate with some of the more, let's say, draining people of my past.

I probably was a bit short with you on a few occasions when you phoned but, to be honest, I don't always have unlimited time to listen to you banging on about how glad you are that you moved to Ipswich. To be clear, I'm happy that it's worked out for you but really feel I don't need to hear the details again and again.

Nor am I captivated by the self-satisfied descriptions you keep

broadcasting about your new 'chilled-out lifestyle'. Being properly chilled out means not feeling the need to tell everyone that
you are chilled out. That is why Keith Richards is so good at it
and everyone on social media isn't.

As for your so-called career change, I accept that picture
framing is of interest to you, but you should know that it is not
something I ever want to be involved in a conversation about.
And since we are being candid, I was pretty alarmed by the photo
you sent everyone of what you described as your workshop. It is
very clearly a garden shed with a bench and some tools scattered
about. Seeing you in your overalls with that little craft hammer
in your hand, well, Sean, the word that sprang to mind was:
pathetic. You look like a seedy version of Pinocchio's dad or one
of those automatons you sometimes see in cobblers' shop windows, except they have more life in their eyes. Speaking of eyes,
is it really necessary to wear those glasses? The round ones with
the bright-red rims. They're new, since moving to Ipswich, aren't
they? You never needed glasses before. I expect you thought they
would make you look talented and sensitive. Instead, they just
shout out, 'Help. I'm having a crisis.'

I am baffled that you put such emphasis on our supposed
'accumulated history', as if we are in some way bound by a shared
past. While it is true that we were at school together, it's also true
that there were more than a thousand other kids at that school,
not one of whom I feel any allegiance towards. And I don't mind
admitting that whenever I have reached out and made contact
with any of them it is pretty clear that the feeling is entirely
mutual. I could have taken that as a rejection and started to

mope around whining about my mental health etc., but no. I'm
made of better stuff than that. I took it on the chin. Yes, I went
back on the Prozac. But I held my head high for the most part.

And yes, I was your best man but that was more than twenty
years ago. Unlike the actual marriage, it is not a lifelong commitment. And as far as organising the stag night is concerned,
I don't think anyone could deny that I did an excellent job. It
cannot be considered my fault that your imbecilic cousin Reece
became overexcited and thought
it would entertain us if he set
fire to the restaurant, bringing
the evening to a premature and
somewhat terrifying end. There
is no way on God's earth I would
have put cocaine in his starter if
I'd known he was such a twat.
Notwithstanding, it was I who
comforted Jean-Pierre and his
wife as their premises got well
and truly flambéed and it was I

> **Seeing you in your overalls with that little craft hammer in your hand, well, Sean, the word that sprang to mind was: pathetic**

who arranged for Reece's mother to stay at the Westgate Ibis
during his trial. Beyond the call, I would say.

Your wedding day itself went pretty well, all things considered.
Even the Revd Maxwell was pretty generous in his support of
my claim that it's all but impossible to guarantee that an item as
small as a ring won't get lost sometimes.

Looking back I probably should have edited my speech to allow
for the somewhat muted atmosphere at the reception, but my

thought at the time was to lighten the mood by really tearing you apart. Hands up, I misread the room and it was obviously never my intention for anyone to go running into the ladies in a state of upset. Least of all the bride. It's a shame Caroline's dad chose that moment to unplug the sound system. I really think that the lads' weekend story of you being arrested by the Spanish police as you dangled by your Y-fronts from a brothel balcony really was hilarious and could well have swung the gig back in my favour.

It came as no surprise of course that you eventually asked Rob and Liz to be godparents to Petal Dew instead of yours truly. (I won't pretend that I wasn't slightly relieved, anyway, not to have to fork out for book tokens for the next eighteen years.) And I also see that my quip that the name Petal Dew sounded like a new type of plug-in air freshener was not well received by either of you.

As for your relocation, I wonder when it was that the seeds of change were sown into your tiny insecure mind? I can well imagine Caroline scouring the internet to see how much more you could get for your money by selling up and moving to a region you knew nothing about. My estimate is it took you less than a full season ticket of commuting to twig that estate agent details are unhelpfully euphemistic and that the description 'Liverpool Street – 90 mins' is a classic example. Was it via a gradual erosion of conceit or a sudden buttock-clenching realisation that you saw you had made a catastrophic mistake? I suspect it was the latter, considering the stink of pure panic that your subsequent career change gave off.

And so there you are, gluing and hammering bits of wood round Vettriano prints and family photos, spending your free time having pops at your old mate and contemplating your mortality as though it is something you are actually looking forward to. You really screwed up, Sean. It's your fault you married Caroline and went on to indulge her every whim. It's your fault you then let her pick a name from a Dulux paint chart for your daughter. It's your fault you couldn't calculate that a commute of ninety minutes = three hours per day trundling around the country in a rickety train carriage that smells of sick. It's your fault you swapped a good job for arsing about, pretending you're a master craftsman on *The Repair Shop* and it's your fault that there is no way back from the dismal netherworld that you've chosen for yourself.

Get lost, Sean. And don't bother replying as I won't be as diplomatic if I have to waste even more of my time writing back.

Addendum

Shortly after the publication of this book it was brought to my attention that the correspondent who wrote to me from Ipswich is not the Sean to whom the reply was addressed. This was an honest mistake and I would like to apologise to that Sean for not dealing with his particular problem. The Sean of my acquaintance, to whom the piece was addressed, contacted me in advance of publication to congratulate me. Sean, mate, if you're reading this, please ignore all that rubbish about your move/life change/wife etc. etc. I was just riffing really. Also, really pleased to hear that Caroline wants to bury the hatchet and for us to get together again. I don't know if that will still be the case when she sees this but, for the record, I'm up for a night out if you both are? Anyway, sorry for the mix-up and love to Caroline and Petal Dew. (That really is a nice name, actually.) Cheers.

> *At 52 I have been single for a number of years now. Although I have been on various dates, they have all been with women that I already knew and none of the dates progressed further than the friendship I already had with them. I am now considering online dating but am nervous of how that might go. Do you have any advice please?*
>
> *Smokey, Redcar*

I very much want to help you with this, Smokey, and I do think I have quite a bit to offer that you should find useful. But first, I would not be doing my job if I didn't deal with the elephant in the room. It's the name thing.

There are a few names that really only one person can ever truly be called and, once that has happened, for a myriad of diverse reasons, the name should not be used ever again. Elvis and Adolf immediately spring to mind. Pelé, Jesus, Morrissey and Myra are all inadvisable first names for parents to choose if they wish to avoid loading their child with unnecessary connotations. Smokey is certainly one such name. Your age suggests to me that your parents were enthusiastic fans of Smokey Robinson, the legendary American singer-songwriter and allowed this to influence what they called you. I could be wrong. They might have been mad about kippers but, on balance, I'm going for the former scenario.

All is not lost, though. Some meet the challenge of a difficult name with alacrity and completely overcome any problems that it might otherwise have caused. Look at Elvis Costello. However, such cases are unusual and in Costello's case it helped that he was prodigiously talented and chose the name for himself in a characteristic mood of wit and irony. Possibly you too have such a talent and will lend the name new resonance with your own gift for songwriting. A surname will be needed if that is the case. Perhaps something British and suggestive of style and grace. Might I suggest 'Smokey Wetherspoon'? The more I repeat it to myself the more I think it smacks of class and sophistication, qualities that will keep a high-end crooner working the clubs until he drops. But I digress; if you are not possessed of a musical gift then I strongly recommend a switch to a new name that promises less and doesn't set up any potential first dates for a crushing disappointment when they ask you to play piano and sing to them.

Which brings us to the subject of your question: online dating and how you should go about it as a novice. My initial thought is that you should not be too daunted – online dating is now extremely commonplace and doesn't carry the stigma that it once did. Of course, as is so often noted, it's only the regrettable cases which make headline news but they are rare indeed. So, for example, I think you'd be exceptionally unlucky to set up a rendezvous with, let us say, Stella from Whitley, only to find she is not Stella from Whitley at all but an itinerant labourer called Stan who has turned up in a stolen Transit van with a duffel bag full of gaffer tape, cable ties and Vaseline. Eight hours later, you find yourself wandering traumatised along the hard shoulder of a motorway with a somewhat jaded opinion of Tinder.

Set aside such concerns and know that, by taking sensible precautions, you don't have to end up in such an unfortunate spot at all. Instead, you might well enjoy a pleasant evening getting to know someone who could just be that special person you were hoping to find. If so, all power to you. This is your time. Let someone else be Stan's bitch and you get on with your life.

You don't have to flick through very many channels on the television nowadays to know that they are awash with dating shows. Mostly these involve a competitive element that sees the contestants being rejected or chosen based on their looks. It is brutal, unromantic and cruel. At times I imagine Charles Darwin pitching the show to Channel 5 in the 1870s. He's explaining the idea to a bunch of really cool TV executives who don't really understand this 'survival of the fittest' craze but are eager to pilot it as soon as television gets invented and programme makers have given up any and all ambition to make quality content.

I offer up this vignette to assure you not to be afraid of superficiality when choosing who to have a date with from pictures and a brief self-penned biog. Nature has hardwired you to do just that – to pick up on the optics – a healthy complexion, physical vigour, strong stature and so on. All these dating apps and websites are but a window display, there to attract your attention and draw you in. It is pure nature that, at this stage, your criteria will be shallow, and that's fine. If you went out to buy a cake and there were two bakeries to choose from, would you go into the one with flies and a couple of week-old apple turnovers in the window or the shop with a window display of beautiful cakes and even a picture of Paul Hollywood holding a Victoria sponge? (OK, bad example.)

Next is the interests section. Here, if you want honesty, then only go with the specific. If someone says that their interests include, for example, breeding iguanas or stock car racing, then it is pretty much guaranteed that that is something they actually do. Because you can't make up a hobby like that. Once you visit their home and say, 'So where are all these iguanas? Can't wait to see them,' they will either show you a room full of iguanas or they won't. If you get an excuse like, 'Oh, they're not here today, they're being used in a TV advertisement for . . . for . . . um, a building society . . .', then you will know: this person is a liar and a fantasist, otherwise why would they come up with such a pathetic story like that? You can then make your excuses and go. (You've got nothing to lose, so why not return the insult and lie yourself? Something like, 'Oh my gosh, I just remembered I have an urgent meeting. I know I didn't put this in my biog, but the fact is I'm a leading architect and I've just remembered I am due at London Zoo because I'm designing a new reptile house for them. Hey, I know, I could design one for you as well – you know, for your iguanas, except you don't have any iguanas, do you? You lying psycho.' And then leg it to the car and get out of there.)

> **If someone says that their interests include, for example, breeding iguanas or stock car racing, then it is pretty much guaranteed that that is something they actually do**

Alternatively, she will have a delightful collection of reptiles and you'll know that here is a person who tells the truth about what she likes and doesn't like. And that is a good start to any relationship.*

When it comes to hobbies and interests, the people you must avoid are the ones who fill this box with totally non-specific activities like walking, reading or cooking. These are all things that most people do every day, regardless. You may as well list emptying the dishwasher, going to the lavatory and breathing. It is not a hobby if you have to do it anyway. So, when you see any of these things listed, what you are really looking at is written proof that this person has had to really thrash around at the bottom of the pastime barrel to find something they can say about themselves, and that is not a good sign. You have to imagine the future and what you hope it will be like. If in ten years' time you say to your partner, 'How was your day?' and the reply is, 'Really good, thanks, I put the bins out and had a dump,' then my hunch is that it will leave you feeling a tad flat.

But supposing you find someone you like the look of and who seems to be compatible with you in enough ways to make you want to take it to the next step and go on a date. Now how should you proceed?

In fact, my advice is to go on a pre-date. Meet for coffee, keep it casual. That way there's much less pressure on both of you for the date to be a 'success'. More importantly though, Smokey – sorry, that name still makes me laugh; in fact I'm just going to call you

---

* I realise, writing this, that the example of breeding iguanas is slightly misleading. As everyone knows, people who keep reptiles for pets are disturbing to be around anyway, so for argument's sake, let us imagine, even though it is unlikely, that this particular hobbyist is otherwise OK company.

Bill from now on – more importantly, Bill, you will know in an instant the disparity between picture and person. As will she.

And if the coffee together is a tiresome flop, then neither of you will have invested much more than half an hour of your time. What could be more dismal than sitting down for an entire three-course meal with someone, only to have to admit to yourself after five minutes you have nothing in common with them? Ask any married couple.

Strangers always think I am grumpy but that is just the way my face naturally hangs. Do you have any advice?

(Via SMS)

First and foremost, I'd caution against corrective procedures. Cosmetic surgeons think they do a good job but that's only because all their patients have to smile forever. Far better to work on actually becoming grumpy so as not to disappoint these strangers. Develop the knack of putting a dampener on everything anyone says to you. For instance, 'Lovely day' should be met with 'Not if you burn easily.' Let's say someone is telling you how great *Peaky Blinders* is – cut them off with, 'I was once attacked by someone in a flat cap from Birmingham so I find the programme traumatising,' and so on.

Dear Jack, My parents are really embarrassing and I am very worried about them ruining my image when I start sixth form next year. At the last parents' evening at my secondary school my mum, who has a really loud and posh voice, called the headmaster 'darling' and said that I 'simply adored' all his lessons (he teaches history, and I don't adore them at all). It didn't matter so much, as I only had a couple of terms left at that school, but I am hoping to reinvent myself at college and really don't want her to ruin everything. There is an open evening for parents at the start of term. How can I stop them from attending?

Aisling, Cardiff

Hi Aisling. I'm very glad that you wrote because, as an embarrassing parent myself, I think I can help add some perspective here. However, I want you to see the full picture because I also was once the mortified offspring that you now are and remember in detail the toe-curling horror of having to be seen with my parents at my school. It was like the collision of two universes that I spent most of my waking hours trying to keep apart from

'It was like the collision of two universes that I spent most of my waking hours trying to keep apart from each other'

each other. And there I was, caught in this gravitational force field of authority, having to answer questions in front of the three worst people I could think of at the time: my parents and (any) teacher. I'm still bitter about the time that Mr Bell, my halitotic maths teacher, said he would be setting me extra homework to help me in my quest to get an O level (which is Anglo-Saxon for GCSE) in the subject. 'Is that a deal?' he said, implying some sort of weird buddy status which he most definitely did not have. 'Is that a deal?' What a wanker.

And of course at that age I had no option but to agree, with a polite and grateful 'Yes sir' – polite and grateful being qualities that I was widely noted in the teaching community for not having. Even as a grown man I still sometimes find myself wishing I had told him where to stick his extra homework but then have to begrudgingly remind myself that he did get me through that exam. Like I say, I wasn't noted for my gratitude. Also, being cursed with a face and vocal intonation that puts sincerity way out of my range, I knew even then that a genuine thank you would have been taken the wrong way.

Another element to your predicament is being seen by your friends with your parents. At a certain stage in anyone's life this can represent a sort of social hara-kiri but you must take reassurance from me on this and know that, without even discussing it beforehand, your entire peer group will have allowed that this particular evening constitutes exceptional circumstances – a kind of existential emergency, if you like – in which all teenage participants are granted amnesty.

The thing to remember is that all parents are embarrassing.

They represent the side of your life that you try your best to keep away from your friends. Most of the time this is possible because you can effectively keep both sides locked in different buildings, i.e. your mum and dad in your house and your friends in school. It is this terrible day-release system whereby your parents are allowed out of their building and into the other one for a few hours that does all the damage.

And my belief is it wouldn't matter who your parents were – this would always be the case. I've often wondered what it would have been like to be the child of really cool people, for instance if one or both of your parents was a rock star. OK, fun for a bit, but my guess is that the novelty would wear off. Yes, you have some of the trappings but could you really say that you are enjoying them? It would be amazing to have a swimming pool but not so amazing when you ask your friends over for a dip one hot afternoon only to discover that you can't actually swim because there's a car in it. 'Why's there a Range Rover in the pool, Aisling? Now we can't go swimming. This party sucks.' And you'd have to just explain. 'I didn't know it was there. My dad must have driven it in.' 'Why would he do a thing like that, Aisling?' 'I dunno. He's just a dick, I guess.' Open evening could well be equally embarrassing with rock star parents, just for different reasons. When your dad turns up smelling of patchouli and wearing more bangles than all the art teachers combined, you might be forgiven for hiding under your fringe and envying the girl called Aisling with the so-called 'normal' parents who are merely loud and excitable.

Or what if your parents are George and Amal Clooney?

Everyone thinks you're so lucky to have such cool parents but soon realise how embarrassing it is for you when your mum threatens to take your English teacher to the supreme court for giving you a C and your dad goes round the hall trying to sell everyone a coffee machine. The thing here is that your parents are not in themselves causing you embarrassment so much as the dynamic between you, them, your teachers, your friends and the wholly unnatural environment you find yourself forced to endure at these school events. So I'd say that it is at least worth recognising that most of us, perhaps especially at your age (sorry, I know that sounds condescending), hate to be put in a position against our will and in which we are unable to present ourselves to our peers as we would wish.

My suggestion is that you would do well to put up with any remaining meetings at the school as graciously as you can. Just tolerate the bullshit and know that there is the prize of sixth form at the end of all this, which is well worth being patient for. When your parents or teachers say, 'We only want what's best for you,' do yourself a favour and nod along. There is no point disputing that, even though it isn't the full truth. Believe me, I understand how tempting it is to say, 'Yes, but you actually only want the best for me because that is what would be best for you. If I do well at school, then it makes your life easier.' However, it is a pointless argument that will achieve almost nothing other than more awkwardness. The only exception would be if your parents and teachers genuinely wanted something harmful for you because they are in a cult and believe you are possessed by the devil. While this can be the case, it is highly unusual and generally ends up as a Netflix documentary, in which case you'd then get your say on a satisfyingly big platform anyway.

Incidentally, you mention that you are hoping to reinvent yourself once you reach sixth form college. Most people reading this will relate to what you say. Moving, whether it be school, home or job usually brings with it the chance to start again with a new circle of contacts and acquaintances. In my line of work, I frequently find myself having to start afresh with different people and yet I consistently fail to come across as likeable to any of them, so possibly I am not best placed to advise you on social skills. In fact I am sure that you will be very popular by being yourself. The fact that I never have been doesn't mean you can't. And possibly you'll discover that, rather than a reinvention, what you need is for your true self to emerge unimpaired by the constraints imposed by a childhood that you have clearly outgrown.

Whatever you decide, Aisling, don't let your parents go on their own. Knowing parents (because I am one), they will probably follow the teacher talk with a trip to a bar afterwards, prolonging your anxiety about what was said and frustrating your enquiries when they do get in because they'll be more than slightly pissed. If you think it's unspeakable that your mother drapes herself adoringly round the headmaster, wait till she comes in and does it to you because your report was better than expected, as were the two bottles of blanc de blancs on the way home.

I am a divorced man of 54. I find that I have put on weight and become quite unfit over the last two or three years which I put down to getting divorced and all the stress that goes with that. I tried to make a big effort at the start of 2020 by joining a fitness class in a park near me but didn't get on with the other people or the instructor, who claimed to be ex-SAS and seemed to dislike me as he never missed an opportunity to show me up. I did start jogging, thinking I might work up to doing a marathon one day but when the lockdown happened I got abused by pedestrians so gave that up as well. I do want to get fit and lose weight but can never find a form of exercise that I like. Your advice would be appreciated.

Warren, Hayes, Middx

Thank you for getting in touch, Warren. It sounds as though you have gone through a lot in the last few years and that, understandably, the pandemic came as the last straw. You were among the millions who started jogging at the beginning of lockdown but whose enthusiasm waned as the weeks rolled by. For some, the decline was even more rapid and exercise had slumped to a masked shuffle to Tesco Express by the time their newly ordered trainers were thrown at the front door by the Amazon courier. When I say 'For some', perhaps I should be more specific and say 'For me'.

I'm sorry to say that I was one of those who responded to the first lockdown with the bolstering belief that we can get through this with grit and courage expressed through physical discipline. I have been a fairly regular jogger for a few years and found it beneficial. The usual distance I would aim for was only about 4k – nothing that was going to break the Fitbit but also nothing that was going to wreck my knees. What I was really after was bragging rights, something to casually drop into conversations – you know, 'when I was out running this morning . . .' type of thing; and 4k is a good exaggeratable distance. I found it lent itself easily to loftier claims of say 8 or even 10k, satisfied that this is not a lie. Not if I include distances from Tuesday and Wednesday. At no point, however, did I ever have the slightest interest in the marathon. Not even when I was watching it, for that matter. Apart from the very mild curiosity generated by the annual question of whether it will be the bloke from Kenya or the bloke from Ethiopia who wins, the only sensation I am aware of feeling while watching the marathon on TV is happiness that I am not doing it. And don't get me started on those amateur runners, many of whom would log impressively quick times – some as little as one minute – before banging on about it at a party.

If by now you are suspecting a thread of hypocrisy woven into this answer, Warren, then let me say that you are only partially correct. Surely I am just as appalling for going on about my feeble daily trots, especially considering the outright mendacity of some of my claims? Surely it is no bad thing to actually complete a marathon, even if you do talk about it a bit too much afterwards? Yes and no. The main difference is that I mention my running so as to fit in, to seem normal, to come across as your average Jack. Whereas marathon runners are fully aware that to complete the course is pretty remarkable* and they are not about to let your encounter with them lack a full account of their heroics, even if it involves that transparent old humble-brag opener, 'So annoying. I finished just over two hours forty-eight – again . . .'

Back to my glittering track and field career. As I have already said, I began lockdown as a regular, fairly keen runner. But then a flyer appeared one day, pasted on a lamp post near my home that read, 'Meet here every morning 6 a.m. for communal fun run.' It struck me as so offensively upbeat and optimistic that I vowed there and then not to run any more.

So it was that I crossed the Rubicon from athlete to pedestrian and was surprised by how swiftly my allegiance shifted. I started to feel irritated that my daily dog walk was being impacted by endless joggers (or super-spreaders as I now called them) pushing past. They seemed unable to slow down or stop, as if my reason for being outside was less valid than theirs and I should stand aside respectfully or expect to be treated like a slalom post as they pushed past, leaving behind a vapour of sweat, puff and noxious emissions for all to inhale. The people of your home town had

---

* Obviously I don't mean those valiant tryers who take twelve hours, because they've never so much as run for a bus before and couldn't be buggered to do any training, don't finish until early the next day and then get interviewed on breakfast television. They are just wasting everyone's time. In fact, call me petty, but I think there is an argument for not allowing them a 'Marathon Finisher' T-shirt. It's not an achievement if the balloons at the finishing line have shrivelled and all the stewards have handed in their hi-vis by the time you get there. Maybe a T-shirt saying, 'I Was a Bloody Nuisance at the Marathon' or 'I Did the Marathon and Even the St John Ambulance People Hated Me by the End' would be more appropriate.

the sense to shout abuse at you, Warren. And you, as the guilty party, had the grace to give up running, for which you deserve great credit.

As for the fitness class, it is not surprising to me that you had difficulties there. Signing up to a twice-weekly public humiliation has never been healthy for anyone and you will doubtless have found the spirited cheeriness of your classmates as tiring as the exercise itself. I could accurately draw a graph that would show a significant attendance drop after a month of this type of class; after two months the truancy is dire enough to resemble the audience at a mime show after the interval. By month three it's magically full again, but only because a new batch of suckers have come forward and paid to be shouted at by a sadist in full battledress.

That brings me to your 'ex-SAS' instructor. The SAS is an elite military task force whose members have a preference for quiet anonymity once they leave their unit. This dignified silence often lasts several weeks or until a book deal and/or a lucrative role on a TV reality show is secured. In some quarters of the British military establishment, using your history with the SAS to secure a television contract is, no doubt, frowned upon. But we the public are generally happy to forgive this transgression in exchange for being able to watch minor celebrities being bru-talised in a Welsh gravel pit.

Perhaps the senior ranks put up with these extracurricular activities in the belief that they promote army life, possibly encouraging young people to consider a future in the armed forces. There are no relevant statistics to hand proving this to be the case but we have to assume that there is at least

Out of breath and aching from the exertion as Rambo screeches 'Why are you here?', you feebly admit 'Sir, because I'm fat, sir.' He asks you why you are fat. 'Sir, because I eat too much, sir

some truth in it. Just as we cannot ignore the likelihood that they also encourage others to go to their nearest army surplus store, get kitted out like Rambo and start a fitness class. Unless he's able to produce irrefutable paperwork to prove otherwise, I think it is safe to say that your instructor belongs to this last group. I am not, for one minute, suggesting that he is unqualified in PE. In fact, I rather suspect he is. Take from that what you will.

What I am saying is that, when looked at in this way, an unavoidable question arises. Why, with a CV that includes special operations in one of the world's most prestigious regiments, would somebody eschew a highly remunerative follow-on career in the media or the private security sector in favour of a life spent goading a bunch of Middlesex lard-arses round a park? (No disrespect.) I think you can see that it doesn't stack up.

You did well to walk away from that class, Warren. Without wishing to leap to conclusions, I'd say he was a fraud and a confidence trickster and I wouldn't be surprised if you read about him one day in the papers when he gets convicted for draining the bank accounts of clients whose trust he had gained. Being unfit and overweight can make you vulnerable and when you're being barked at while desperately trying to do squat jumps, you'll

answer any question just for the noise and pain to stop. Out of
breath and aching from the exertion as Rambo screeches 'Why
are you here?', you feebly admit 'Sir, because I'm fat, sir.' He asks
you why you are fat. 'Sir, because I eat too much, sir.' Without you
noticing, the questions change course slightly – 'What is your
date of birth?' – and you oblige. 'What is your mother's maiden
name?' Unthinkingly you answer the tyrant: 'Sir, Taylor with a
Y, sir.' Then he suddenly says, 'Now hand me your smartphone
and take your miserable bloated butt three times round the field.'
And before you can say 'defibrillator', you're crawling the second
lap as he transfers your savings into his offshore account.

You finish your letter by asking me if I can help you find a
form of exercise that you like. To which I say: no, I can't. Because
there isn't one. Sorry, Warren, between us we have more than a
hundred years of trying and failing in that quest. I have nothing
constructive to suggest. All I can do is sympathise. I know
how hard and frustrating it is every single time you try, to be
confronted by the realisation that your goals are unachievable
without extreme, prolonged effort and sacrifice. There is no quick
route to weight loss that does not involve dieting and exercise –
with the possible exception of amputation, which as a strategy
is not without its negatives. I really feel that the most I can do
is to help you avoid wasting time on some of the other keep-fit
activities I have attempted.

A lot of people swear by yoga. I tend to swear during it. I
cannot think of a worse way to spend time than in a yoga class.
During lockdown, I did some Zoom sessions accompanied by
my wife, who is a regular practitioner and thought it might be

beneficial for me. How wrong she was. The only thing I was any good at was the bullshit meditation bit at the end and that was because the sitar music sent me straight to sleep. The rest of the class was a sequence of impossible contortions while being told by the instructor – sorry, 'yogi' – how good each position was for various ailments and emotions. By the third time she said, 'This is particularly good for all that anger,' I spluttered that I wasn't fucking angry, crawled out of shot and went and got myself a cold beer from the fridge. My conclusion? Yoga is a Hindi word meaning 'Thin people showing off'. Take your mat and shove it.

Tennis is another inexplicably popular activity. Wonderful to watch when being played well, but relentlessly cruel to the newcomer on court. Plus it involves human interaction and I maintain that pretty much the only nice thing about exercise is not having to do it with other people.

You are now of an age at which you could legitimately consider walking football. I've never tried it myself but am drawn to the idea as it is an undeniably comical concept. It can be viewed as a walk for people who don't have anywhere to go, or as a game of football for people who aren't that fussed about getting the ball. Either way, the thought of it makes me smile and I look forward to hearing how that works out for you, should you decide to take it up.

I hope that I have been able to help, Warren. To summarise, I think you did well to get away from Shambo and his acolytes. You did the right thing there. Be honest with yourself. There is no shame in not being sporty; in fact, it's a trait that should be celebrated. Having little or no interest in exercise frees up time and forces you to be more creative. Of course being healthy is important and keeping fit is an obvious part of that. The key is to find a way of doing less for more gain and not being press-ganged into activities that you hate and are only doing because of social pressure. Exercising in public is a form of passive fat-shaming that spreads guilt to all onlookers. Turn away, avert your eyes and get on with your life.

> *Dear Jack, I am keen on DIY but my long-term partner Gail pre-*
> *fers to pay professionals to do simple jobs around the house which*
> *I feel I could do myself and are well within my capability. This is*
> *causing arguments as I feel that I can, for the most part, do just*
> *as good a job as the professionals but she insists I do not and that*
> *I take too long. Please can you advise as to how to deal with this?*
> *Warwick, Chester*

Warwick, as I see it, there are two forces acting against each other here. The first is your partner's desire to have odd jobs and maintenance work around the house completed to a high standard with minimum disruption. Then the second force, which, as I say, is in conflict with the first, is that you see these tasks as: (a) well within your capability; (b) your duty to personally complete; and (c) something you enjoy doing as you are keen on DIY.

So I will take those three thoughts in order.

(a) Well within your capability ('for the most part', as you put it). Setting aside the qualifying remark that you have added, the phrasing of your self-assessment is unsettling in a way that I don't think you have grasped. When a tradesman claims that something is 'well within my capability', it immediately causes concern because wherever there is a 'within' there must also be a 'without'. What he is actually saying is that there is a defined list of tasks that he is capable of and a similar list of things that he is not capable of – and that he *thinks* the task he has been asked to do is on the can-do list.

You might argue that this is ungenerous of me and that the tradesman is being humble, rather than showing incompetence. Either way, it doesn't matter because the damage has been done; that seed of doubt has been sown. The householder will now be thinking, 'Can he actually do this, or should I read into his statement that there is a reasonable possibility that he will make an utter botch of it and I will electrocute myself the first time I use the dishwasher? Can he fit floorboards or will I fall through them like a clown at a circus after he's gone home to count his cash? Is he, in fact, a qualified plumber who knows how to install a toilet, or is he basically figuring it out as he goes along, meaning that I could well walk into the bathroom next morning, slip in a pool of leaking soiled water and crack my head on the side of the bath?'

If you are still not convinced, ask yourself how relaxed you would be, taxiing on the runway in an airliner and you hear over the speaker system: 'Good afternoon, this is your first officer speaking. We'll shortly be taking off and climbing to a cruising altitude of 34,000 feet. Don't worry, I know that sounds tricky but it is well within my capability. For the most part.'

Or the sense of panic if a surgeon says to you, just as you're being wheeled into the operating theatre, 'Nothing to worry about, Warwick. Pretty sure I can do this, despite last time. Count backwards from ten, please.'

These examples should help you see that, at the very least, you have not sold yourself well to Gail in respect of your DIY skills. With your self-effacing choice of words, you thought you were coming across as frank and honest, but to Gail, you were actually coming across as Frank Spencer.

(b) You consider these tasks your duty to personally complete. Well, that's a maybe. The problem is that Gail doesn't. You should be thankful for that. Your girlfriend is clearly no sexist and doesn't expect you to do, or be able to do, these jobs just because you are a man. Let yourself off the hook; she has. Next time the two of you want a new shelf built, relax, open a can of beer and let her google 'reliable carpenters near me' (I guarantee a picture of you will not come up, which should tell you something). Put bluntly, if that shelf collapses, smashing the lovely tea set Gail's granny left her, who do you want to get the blame – you or the 'professional' that she organised? Exactly. 'Never take responsibility for things you don't have to' is a rule by which I live my life and I recommend it to you (although I would add that I did not write the rule and you adopt it at your own risk). You might be thinking about the cost element but you really shouldn't. By the time you've wasted a morning going out and buying the exact tools and materials you need, you're already losing money. Then include the hours spent doing the 'home improvement' instead of working at your real job that you get paid to do. And that's not even factoring in that moment when you've finally finished your handiwork after several tense hours of measuring, cutting, drilling, screwing, and then redoing all the above: she arranges the tea set on the new shelf and you both stand back, you admiring your cabinetry; then she says 'Is it straight?' Three little words that somehow compel you to take a hammer to her 'stupid, stinky old granny's teapot'. And then you really would be in the shit, wouldn't you, Warwick?

(c) You say that you are keen on DIY. I question how genuine that is and wonder whether it is not more the case that you hanker after Gail's approval. Your letter suggests you believe that even if the result of your handiwork is sub-standard, the good intent deserves some praise at least. This attitude accounts for why nearly every fridge door in the country is bedecked with our children's artwork. However, sometimes even the most doting parent will look at her darling one's latest offering and have to bin it. Mum can see that, even for a three-year-old, it's a mindless scribble, dashed off in the hope of more adulation and possibly a biscuit. It is quite obvious that the toddler's manic crayoning is a sort of primitive commercial ploy and that when he says, 'I drew a picture for you, Mummy,' what he really means is, 'Can I have a Jaffa Cake?'

Now is the time to ask yourself whether you have become an adult version of that toddler. Constantly seeking reward by delivering shoddy, unwanted work. The mother reminds me of Gail and the point she has reached regarding you and your DIY. She is no longer even pretending to be pleased with your attempts and has come to the conclusion that it is harmful to your relationship, not to mention the house, to encourage you. I know that it is hard for you to hear this, Warwick, but any praise she initially might have given was a sort of fake orgasm, acted out in the hope that your performance would improve. You may be enjoying things but she isn't, which explains why she craves a proper builder.

However, there is some light at the end of the tunnel. My reputation in the field of counselling wouldn't be what it is were it not for my positivity and unique gift for building people up. In the realm of psychotherapy, making someone feel even worse than when they approached you for help is the indisputable mark of a charlatan. And I think that everyone reading this will agree that I am no charlatan.

So the light at the end of the tunnel? I suggest you become a professional odd-jobber in your spare time. That way you can fulfil your craftsman fantasies but do so by wrecking other people's homes, not Gail's. From what I can glean you are easily good enough to go pro. Let's face it, it's a low bar. It's pretty obvious that, in this country anyway, all you need in order to go around calling yourself a tradesman is not to be in prison that day. You are more than qualified to set yourself up in business this way. It really is the perfect solution. It allows you to trade in cash only – tax free – drive a van and eat sausage rolls anytime you want to, not just at Christmas like normal people. Gail will be happy because you are satisfying your need to use power tools somewhere that she never has to see the horrible results. The advantages are almost limitless and far outweigh the occasional doorstepping by some busybody daytime TV show like *Cowboy Builders*, poking around trying to find out why you fitted a gas boiler in a nursing home when you aren't Corgi-registered. 'So what if it's leaking? So are all the residents,' you blurt as your hand smothers the cameraman's lens and you push past that little bald bloke with the microphone and leg it down the road. Good luck, Warwick. See you on the telly.

Dear Jack, We strictly limit television and computer time as we want our children to play outdoors and to read books instead of just sitting staring at a screen. Now they never seem to be at home. Are we being unreasonable? They don't seem to appreciate that we have their best interests at heart.

Kadeesha, London

Dear Kadeesha, you don't say the age of your children but, as they now spend much of their time away from home, I am going to estimate that they are of secondary-school age. It would appear that your strategy to get your children away from the television and computer has backfired. Instead of meekly complying and immersing themselves in a novel, they have prematurely begun the process of separation from you. For the record, I think your instinct to limit screen time is an understandable one and I do get a high volume of correspondence on this issue. However, in your case, things have gone too far in the other direction and I can see that it is important for you to reset and bring things closer to your ideal of family life.

Before moving on to what your children are getting up to, I want to deal with the book/screen thing. Please don't worry about their lack of interest in reading. A love of reading among young people is increasingly rare. Of course in the last few years there has been a spike in children's literature – largely down to the phenomenal sales of J.K. Rowling – but I would contend that the purchase of a book does not equate with the reading of that book. Practically before anyone had got through the first chapter of *The Philosopher's Stone*, the film was released, meaning the book was hastily flung aside in anticipation of a trip to the cinema. Inevitably, after having seen the film, most kids would confidently declare that they had read the book. Adults were not innocent of this either, although their real crime, ironically, *was* to read the book. One of the more sickening sights of the early noughties (and yes, I hate that word as much as you do) was that of grown men and women reading the latest Harry Potter instalment in public, apparently with no embarrassment at all. Just sitting there, on the train, bus or park bench, devouring stories about people with wands and magic broomsticks. In part, this is testament to Rowling's genius. Crossing that age-group chasm is something Enid Blyton never achieved. At least, I am assuming that she never achieved it; it's certainly a challenge to imagine those grizzled post-war commuters puffing away on their pipes, brolly on arm, with the latest Famous Five adventure in hand. It's a generational thing. My working assumption is that once you've flown a Spitfire in battle, escaped from Colditz and cracked the Enigma code it would be hard to give a monkey's toss about a bunch of nine-year-olds helping the police by trapping some travelling tinker in a cave after he was seen pinching apples. And the less said the better about that foaming-at-the-mouth eugenicist, Noddy, and his Gypsy-hating friend Big Ears.

However, it is more than just a testament to Rowling, it also speaks to one of the defining characteristics of twenty-first-century adults, namely an inability to grow up. And if you don't believe me, why do so many kids riding around doing stunts on BMXs have beards? It makes no sense unless you allow that they are, on a psychological level, trying to atone for a childhood spent on screens.

Of course things were different for my generation. I grew up in the sixties and seventies (but we lived in the countryside, so really I grew up in the fifties). Obviously the only screens we knew were the television, the Odeon and that thing in the car that you'll go through face first if you don't listen to nice Jimmy Savile and clunk-click every trip.

Television for me as a kid was a meagre diet of *Blue Peter*, *Wacky Races* and *The High Chaparral*. As a result, I still can't throw away wire coat hangers without wanting to bend them into one of John Noakes's lethal Advent candelabras complete with real burning candles (surely the original twisted firestarter). In addition, I cheat in competitions to a level that would make Muttley blush, have twelve points on my driving licence and have been cautioned by the police for attempted horse rustling. Technically, the last of these was attempted shoplifting from Tony's Toy Animal Kingdom in Southampton, but I was only nine, was dressed as a cowboy and called the officer 'Sheriff' throughout the questioning, so feel the charge upgrade is earned.

> **Obviously the only screens we knew were the television, the Odeon and that thing in the car that you'll go through face first if you don't listen to nice Jimmy Savile and clunk-click every trip**

Watching TV was by appointment only and so, inevitably, we watched less of it. This was no virtuous choice – if nothing was on, nothing was on. We were forced to do other things. We used our imagination; for instance we'd imagine one day banging on and on to young people about how we had to make our own entertainment when we were their age. I am being facetious because I don't want to sound like one of those disapproving bores, claiming to have filled their childhood with wondrous creativity and inventiveness. If so inclined, a few children of every generation may do exactly that, but for the rest of us, youth is about striking a delicate balance between lethargy and mania.

Kadeesha, you are doing no harm by imposing a screen ban in the home but it is possible you are not doing that much good either. Therefore I'd suggest easing up on this quite strict regime, especially if the corollary of it is that you don't know where your kids are or what they are up to. It would be an unkind irony if, as the result of your vigilant parenting, your sons and daughters are 'down the rec' glue-sniffing or couriering satchel-loads of crack around the country for a local teenage drug baron. Perhaps a bit of give and take would help alleviate your anxiety and make them more likely to want to be at home. Life now for that generation is probably harder than it has ever been in peacetime modern Britain. In just the last few years we have all had to grapple with the catastrophe of Covid-19 and the divisiveness of Brexit. Then Steps announced their reunion coupled with a new album. The suffering just goes on and on, so we need to be kind to ourselves and each other. Thank you for writing and good luck, Kadeesha.

My problem, Jack, is that people seem to ignore me. At the company where I have worked for fourteen years almost nobody seems to know my name. I don't know what I can do to develop some sort of charisma so that people pay a little bit more attention to me. As someone who has spent so much time on stage I wondered if you might have any tips for me? Thank you.

(Via SMS)

Hello Jack, a few years ago I told a lie which I have had to uphold ever since. I told my parents that I work in banking when in fact I am a travelling insurance rep. I think that I originally started this because there was a long-standing joke in my family about insurance salesmen being the lowest of the low. When I left university it was the only job I could get but I felt insecure about telling my parents, so I fibbed, intending to put it right a few months later by saying I had been head-hunted and so switched careers. However, that moment never came and now I have to read up on banking jargon so I can maintain the pretence and meanwhile the insurance salesman jokes and insults keep flying around whenever we are all together. Siobhan, my wife, knows about this and although she won't actually lie, finds ways of not dumping me in it when we are all together. But now my kids are getting to an age when they ask about my work so I want to stop all this pretending and come clean but don't know where to start. Can you help, Jack?

Jim, Aberdeen

Hello Jim. From your description I can see that this is a one-off problem that has mushroomed from a single lie. Let me say right from the outset that, should this develop into a pattern of repeat lying, then you may need to seek help on a one-on-one basis so that you can gain a better understanding of why you might be experiencing such urges. Be under no illusion: compulsive lying can indicate underlying personality disorders which should always be referred for appropriate treatment. That is, in fact, why I founded the Royal Society for the Treatment of Liars, whose head office is in Nantwich and whose patron is none other than HRH Prince Michael of Kent, a very dear friend of mine. Obviously all of that is a lie. In fact, if I am to be scrupulously honest, I will admit that it's a lie that is trying to be a joke.

Now, at this point, you could be forgiven for being cross that I have made a cheap swipe at your expense. Actually, I included it to highlight one of the main problems we encounter when talking about lying, namely that our inability to know what is and is not true in a conversation on the subject becomes, inevitably, comical unless we first establish some ground rules. That is why it is important to establish this is a single deception rather than a more problematic compulsion. Unless that is settled, we might very well go round and round in existential circles, never really surfacing from the downward pull of 'Doctor, Doctor' jokes.*

It would also be good to look briefly at some of the different categories of dishonesty that exist, as I believe this will give you some helpful perspective. For our purposes, we only need

---

* For readers abroad who are unfamiliar with 'Doctor, Doctor' jokes, they are short and silly gags based on the doctor/patient relationship in which the patient's response to the doctor's question often confirms the ailment. In this particular case you might expect the likes of: 'Doctor, Doctor, I can't stop lying' – 'When did this start?' – 'When I won a gold medal for pole vaulting at the Beijing Olympics.' NB: nowhere did I say they were funny.

to consider the less serious of these (1–4). (In case you are interested, dishonesty categories 5, 6 and 7 are: Compulsive, Pathological and – the most serious – Should Be in Prison, which in my opinion, applies to Vinnie's Quality Used Phones and Laptops on the Edgware Road). So, here are the types of lie that concern us:

1. The Harmless Voluntary Lie (HVL). This is the least problematic of all lies and the sort that almost all of us use and encounter on a daily basis. Often it features in our conversation as exaggeration and so can be used rhetorically and without unfortunate consequences. Let's suppose that you have just come back from the supermarket and you say to Siobhan, 'It was a right scrum at the fish counter,' she will immediately understand the reference and treat it as a description that is not literally true. Nearly all of us would be able to discern that as being a colourful way of saying how busy it was without making the mistake of believing that a game of rugby was taking place at the fish counter. In other instances, the HVL will be what is referred to as a 'white lie'. Let's imagine your parents have taken you out for a meal to celebrate your birthday. You might be asked by a waiter, while they are paying, if you enjoyed your meal. You tell him enthusiastically that you did, even though it was, truth be told, absolute filth. You have technically told a lie but only because you didn't want to upset your mother and father after they had been so generous. Also, it certainly wasn't their fault that your shepherd's pie was fridge-cold in the centre and the veg

appeared to have been left to boil since the end of the war, so why make them feel bad about it?

2. Next up is the Everyday Lie (EL). This is not dissimilar to the above but is considered more serious because of its greater potential for causing complications and/or becoming habit forming. As with the HVL, this type of lie is frequently regarded as innocuous but often lacks any motive or justification, which can be distressing for the perpetrator who is left wondering why they needed to lie. An example of this might be when, in response to the question 'Have you seen the new James Bond film?', you say that you have, even though you haven't. Perhaps you've seen the trailer and read a review and felt confident enough to make the claim, believing that would make you appear more cool or clever or, well, the fact is you don't know what. But of course it doesn't make you appear anything in particular – not yet, anyway. It results in you having to continue an entirely false conversation and becoming increasingly tense and eager to change the subject before your lie becomes problematic and your companion says something like, 'Annoyingly, I had a text to say there was a crisis at work, so I had to leave the cinema ten minutes before the end. What happened?' This leaves you fumbling and spluttering about how you wouldn't be able to find the words to do it justice, adding, 'especially the explosion. I was so relieved when it turned out he wasn't dead after all', feeling sure that they were safe details to add. But no, your explanation is met with a silent stare, until you feel obliged to admit that you haven't seen the film and that you have absolutely no idea why

you said you had. Everyday Lies don't always end awkwardly like that, but they nearly always have an uncomfortable air of pointlessness about them. So, you might be asked what you had for breakfast and, knowing you had cornflakes, announce that you had kippers. The lie doesn't actually matter. Probably nobody will ever know it was a lie. It's just that you spend the rest of the day in a mild state of unease with yourself, wondering why you said that.

3. The Fantasist Lie (FL) takes the Everyday Lie to the next level. Unlike the comparatively inconsequential fibs that all of us tell from time to time, the FL involves a conscious fabrication of events, people and places. It marks a descent into a fictitious existence that, left unchecked, can cause havoc in whoever's lives it touches. An example that I came across not long ago was of a cat that went missing. The owner asked her neighbour if he had seen the cat. Instead of telling the truth that he had not, he said that he had seen the cat being picked up by an Eastern European-looking gentleman who put it in his van and drove off. The worried owner asked her neighbour if he had managed to get a registration number, to which he said he wasn't able to as it had sped off so fast, but that it was a blue van with 'SLAVIK'S QUALITY FUR COATS' written on the side. Here was a clear case of a completely unnecessary falsehood that caused needless distress. Happily the cat reappeared soon afterwards and the neighbour was left having to explain his story to the owner's husband. You would have thought that an apology would have closed the matter, but not at all, there followed a scuffle in which the lying neighbour received a

black eye which is still sore and only just starting to go down as I write this. A timely lesson for whoever that person was in how an FL, told more or less as a joke, can quickly escalate into a violent incident.

4. Next on the mendacity rundown is the One-Off Whopper (OOW). So far this is the gravest form of lying on the list. Typically, the OOW consists of a lie to a person or group of persons that is significant enough in content and magnitude to remain active for a considerable length of time, sometimes years, and so requires constant vigilance from the liar if his/her deceit is not to be uncovered. Another characteristic of this kind of lie is that the pain far outweighs the gain – a classic situation in which the lie is seen to be a good way to deal with an issue but turns out to make everything worse than the problem it was meant to solve. To be honest with you, Jim, we need look no further than your very own case for a gold standard example of the OOW. It's easy to understand your intentions when you told your parents that you had a job in banking: it would spare you the awkwardness of breaching something that is, in your family anyway, a taboo. And it meant that you could enjoy your parents' company, free of their deadening disappointment at how you had underachieved in their view. It's easy now to see that a frank conversation in the beginning could have prevented all the subsequent angst for you, Siobhan and soon, your children. But there was never a truer or more quoted aphorism than 'hindsight is a wonderful thing'. If only its author had had the foresight to copyright it.

The next question that we should address is whether or not your parents have actually twigged that you are not a banker and you are in fact an insurance salesman. It's worth examining whether you have ever inadvertently given them any clues that you have been lying through your teeth for years. In broad brushstrokes, then, the signs that someone is lying fall into two categories: content and delivery.

'Content' pertains to what is actually being said. We have probably all been in situations in which, having been deceived, we reconsider what was actually said to us and realise that there were clues we could have picked up on had we been more alert. As a rule, it is always worth considering how conveniently somebody's narrative fits their own purposes.

For example, a builder arrives at my house. Let's say his name is Derick and he has come to retile my bathroom floor, but he is two hours late, which is pretty annoying for starters. If he says, 'Sorry I'm late, Jack. I overslept because I had too much to drink last night. I'll make it up by working late if that suits you. Once again, apologies – unprofessional of me. Shouldn't have happened,' then I would think that that was fair enough. Why? Well, the reason he has given is not one that a liar would make up because it makes his transgression worse by adding drunkenness to the original offence of being late.

A lying builder, however, would say: 'Sorry I'm late, Jack, the little 'un woke up with a spot of earache so we had to take her to A & E. I would have rung only I was so worried I forgot my phone, so the wife took her home and I came straight here . . .' As most people know already, I'm an easy-going type so would probably say, 'No worries, Derick. I hope she's OK. Let me know if you need to leave early, won't you?' Then I'd put aside my irritation, convince myself that the builder is a virtuous, caring family man and that I should even be grateful he has prioritised my bathroom floor when he has a sick child at home. Until, that is, I take him his statutory cup of tea (four sugars, for Christ's sake – he might as well have checked himself in at the diabetes clinic while he was at the hospital) and catch a glimpse of myself in the mirror, where for a fleeting moment I am convinced I see myself with two massive donkey ears sprouting from my head. He was lying. Of course he was. None of what he said could have been true. Not one word of it. He's even got his paint-splattered phone with him now, despite leaving it at home and coming straight here, according to his bullshit sob story. What a bitter pill that is for me to swallow. To discover that my generous display of care and sympathy was elicited by a cynical web of deceit, spun around the cathedral of good nature that is my personality.

If only I had looked more closely at the content of his opening statement when he arrived, I might have avoided this awful sense of violation, as well as saved myself a kilo of sugar. Revisited, it's easy to spot the clues in Derick's 'excuse'. I will ignore the troubling fact that, despite the numerous NHS campaigns explaining that ailments such as earache are neither an accident nor an emergency, Derick and his wife felt that the right course of action was to bypass the appropriate response of calling 111 for advice, asking a pharmacist for help or even going to their GP. Being stupid is different from being a liar. Just look at how honest the judges on *The X Factor* are. The very obvious inconsistency in Derick's account is that nobody, since the founding of the National Health Service in 1948, has ever been seen, treated and discharged by A & E in two hours.

Applying this criterion to the lie you told your parents would help to indicate the lie's plausibility as far as they are concerned. Could it be that they thought something wasn't quite right and that your claim that you work in the giddy world of banking was inconsistent with the cheap suit and obvious fleet car that you had started to go around in? Were you careful enough not to mention the numerous Travelodges you have to stay at, or your intimate knowledge of every motorway service station in Britain? It's surprising how much is revealed by an innocent remark like, 'Markham Vale's just a petrol station with a Macca drive-thru whereas Donington's got Greggs, Krispy Kreme, Burger King – the lot.' Is that so, George Soros? Certainly, if they have concluded that you are living a lie, the urgency to explain and correct the matter becomes all the more acute.

> **The very obvious inconsistency in Derick's account is that nobody, since the founding of the National Health Service in 1948, has ever been seen, treated and discharged by A & E in two hours**

Let us now move on to the second sign of lying: 'delivery'. Very often, we don't need to be as forensically sharp as I was in the above examples. A simpler method is to train one's ear for the telltale phrases frequently used by the compulsive liar. This table lists some common examples:

PHRASE	TYPE	MEANING
Can I be honest with you?	Preamble	What I am about to tell you should be regarded as an admission that I have, until now, been dishonest with you and yet I nevertheless labour under the deluded idea that I deserve to be believed when I speak.
To be completely honest . . .	Preamble or postscript	*Complete* honesty is such an unusual mode for me that it is noteworthy. NB. If placed at the end of a sentence, it means that even the speaker realises that what he has just said is palpable nonsense and that he is actually so desperate that he sees no choice other than to double down on it.
The truth is . . .	Preamble	Usually I lie through my teeth but not now . . . (if you can believe that).
I'm not going to lie . . .	Preamble	I am about to lie . . .
. . . sort of thing.	Postscript	I know my explanation is implausible. That's because it isn't strictly truthful and I'm covering myself with this feeble expression, hoping that I come across as merely vague rather than rotten to the core of my being.
. . . if you know what I mean.	Postscript	. . . because I don't. I'm so used to talking garbage I've lost track of what's true and what isn't.
. . . guv.	Postscript	I'm hoping that mockney subservience will trick you into thinking that I'm a salt-of-the-earth type who tells it like it is. But the truth is I'm a lying sack of tomtit and think I can get away with it by talking like someone who's escaped from a musical.*

* The aforementioned Vinnie of Vinnie's Quality Used Phones and Laptops on the Edgware Road used all the above and in my opinion is probably the most dishonest electronics trader in the UK. Had the laptop I bought from him in good faith actually been fit for purpose, this book would have been in the shops for Christmas 2020. Months of hard work, not to mention £120 (cash) that I will never see again. What an absolute wanker he is.

As well as these giveaway phrases, 'delivery' also relates to the mannerisms and body language of the speaker, which to the experienced observer can be read like subtitles. Once aware of what to look for, beginners in this art often report that reading body language has more to do with identifying and respecting the accuracy of your instincts than it does with learning a new skill. Consider the way we might automatically perceive shiftiness in someone because they avert their gaze too often when looked at. That is not a learnt conclusion but an atavistic impulse – an inherited memory of not trusting a predator whose sideways glances were to ensure that we were unaccompanied and therefore easy prey. You can see good examples of this on David Attenborough's *Blue Planet* and if you go to buy a used car.

When people fidget and display general restlessness while speaking it can be taken as a reliable sign of lying. It is as if they have channelled all their tension into a twitch or exaggerated hand movements. It's one reason why people waving for help as they are swept away in tidal estuaries are so often not taken seriously.*

It should be said that it is also a common mistake to think that if someone is very still while speaking they must be telling

---

* No doubt some readers will think that this refers to the tabloid report of 1998 that I simply stood back and let a twelve-year-old Girl Guide rescue a distressed swimmer from the River Severn. It doesn't and I can categorically state that the piece was incorrect. She was thirteen, had a life-saving badge and was clearly capable of coping by herself. The last thing she would have wanted was me stealing her thunder. That was my thinking at the time and still is. The fact that the local press chose to describe me as a 'gibbering coward' is more a reflection of that paper's disrespect for accuracy than of my personality.

the truth. Sometimes, stillness is the result of an over-awareness that the body transmits information that we wish to conceal and so the speaker compensates in a way that, ironically, can inform us of their thinking. In that sense, a serene composure can be a type of physical double bluff. More seriously, stillness is displayed because the speaker is completely devoid of any moral fibre or emotional pulse and is so cognitively disconnected from what they are saying that it doesn't even register in their body language. This explains the cold demeanour of psychopaths when they are on trial. And of Vinnie at Vinnie's Quality Used Phones and Laptops on the Edgware Road.

However, nothing that you have relayed to me in your email suggests that you will have incorporated any of these obvious giveaway signals in your behaviour towards your parents over the years. Indeed, had you done so, I suspect that, by now, they would have said something. Therefore, I think that we should approach the matter of your future strategy and resolution on the assumption that your parents were not aware and remain unaware of your deception. This means that you really have two options to consider.

The first is that you simply tell them that you have switched careers. You tell them that you hadn't said anything before because you are aware that the position of insurance salesman is considered by them to be laughable, but the fact is that you are happy in your 'new' job and suggest that the family finds someone else to laugh at next Christmas. Maybe poor people or chiropodists – anyone, so long as it's not you. However, there is the danger in this that, rather than solving your problem, you will be compounding it with what is, let's face it, another lie. What you really want is to be able to be at ease with your parents and free from the fear of being discovered to have lied to them. And therefore, my advice to you is as follows.

You can arrange a time and place to meet with your parents, telling them you have something you wish to tell them. It may seem cynical, but wording your request in this way deliberately creates in your parents a sense of dread. The more their minds are set spinning with imagined disclosures of the gravest and most shaming nature – the big three in their eyes being bankruptcy, divorce and having a Matalan account – the easier they will be to win over with the comparatively innocuous truth that you are about to tell them. Remember as you go about this that much of your reticence is tied to the relationship that you have with your parents. (I don't wish to sully my work by quoting potty-mouth poet Philip Larkin but he does at least make the good point that parents make mistakes when bringing up their children and that those mistakes can have long-lasting consequences. If only he could have put it in so many words.) Therefore, it would be a good idea to rehearse what you say so that you can be controlled and articulate when you meet, rather than regressing into mumbling-child mode as soon as you see them, only to chicken out with something like, 'Oh, it was nothing really . . . I was thinking . . . of getting a pressure washer to do the patio and wondered if you rate that one you've got. Not that I'll have time to use it, probably, as I'm so busy, you know, at the bank, to be completely honest . . .'

In fact, Jim, I have every confidence that you will have no

trouble in explaining the truth about your career and that your intense relief at having finally told the truth will be equally shared by your mother and father as they learn that you are *not* there to tell them that you need emotional support, practical assistance or money from them. Trust me, as a parent that's always what I want to hear first of all. Once that's out of the way, I'm happy to help. Good luck, Jim.

Each year I find myself having to pay for bigger and bigger birthday parties for our twins. Last year my wife took them and all their friends to a theme park, the year before it was Marwell Zoo and this year they want a magician to come to the house. How can I get them to lower their sights and not expect so much?

(Via SMS)

Bloody kids, eh? Don't worry, they'll soon grow out of it and will be asking for cash instead of conjurers. Next thing you'll know, the cops will be at your door saying they've been nicked for selling crack and they're the worst thing that's happened to the neighbourhood since the Krays.

> *Hi Jack, I've been with my husband for 20 years, married for 14. We've always had quite a good sex life, but over the last couple of years he seems to have completely gone off sex. I'm wondering whether I should try to spice things up but am worried about embarrassing myself. What do you think?*
>
> *(Via SMS)*

I think there are two possible explanations here: he could be having an affair or he might have an undiagnosed serious illness. Obviously if the former is true you will be hoping the latter is as well. By all means try to spice things up but take things slowly if you want to avoid the embarrassment that you mention. Don't suddenly appear at the bedroom door wearing a gimp mask and strap-on dildo and telling him to 'prepare for punishment'. I don't mind telling you that something similar happened to me in a relationship many years ago and my right ankle has never fully recovered from landing badly from her third-floor window.

> Hi Jack. In the last few years I have noticed a definite increase in political arguments at dinner parties etc. I personally find this tedious and wondered if you have any tips on how to steer the conversation back to other subjects?
>
> Fran, Leicester

Hello Fran. Well, we are living in turbulent times, aren't we? As I write these words I have one ear primed for updates on how many people I am allowed to socialise with. Only a few months ago I would have had to be on probation, married to a control freak or living in North Korea to make that statement, but no, I am in the UK, nervously praying that there won't be another run on toilet roll, if you know what I mean. My publishers have said that from reading the first draft they fully expect this book to go international.* For that reason, I will include in my answer to you a brief resumé of British politics for the benefit of the many foreigners who will no doubt be reading this.

The story of our country has reached a cliffhanger moment as the various plots now converge to create what promises/

---

* Allow me to say that when I tweeted this prediction I didn't appreciate the responses I received along the lines that 'yes, the book will go international . . . on a barge to a furnace in Malaysia'. I'm not angry or bothered by it. I just feel sorry for you. All 476 of you.

threatens to be an extraordinary climax. It has come to a pretty pass when the returning TV series *Spitting Image* struggles not to be upstaged and out-laughed by real events. One can almost imagine the puppets coming alive when the studio is dark, *Toy Story*-style, and rolling about in tears of laughter watching the *News at Ten*.

(Notice how presumptuously I use the term 'UK' in my opening paragraph. There is absolutely no guarantee that, by the time you read these words, the United Kingdom will not be an etymological relic of the early twenty-first century. It could well be that the Scottish National Party will get their way and gain a second once-in-a-lifetime referendum and achieve the result that they want instead of the annoying, wrong result that the Scottish electorate delivered.)

Therefore, it shouldn't be surprising that social conversation is dominated by the constantly changing situation in which we find ourselves today. You don't need me to tell you, Fran, that in England at least we have three main political parties: Conservative, Labour and the BBC. Until only recently there were also the Liberal Democrats but they made the classic comedy move of electing a leader who promptly lost her seat, thus catapulting her party on its path from rags to ruin. All very sad, but at the same time utterly compelling viewing, like when Oasis split up, although Oasis had more members.

The Labour Party is the Doctor Who of British politics: every time you think it has died, it morphs into its next incarnation. Recently, in the 2019 general election, we saw the Doctor, played by kindly Jeremy Corbyn, lose a well-fought battle against his arch enemy the Daleks – or the public, as we call them. It was quite a cliffhanger; just as the Doctor uttered his last words about free internet and his plucky assistant John began to cry into his manifesto, the credits rolled, that familiar whirly music played and we had to wait five months for the next series to find out who the new Doctor would be. But it was worth the wait. Fans of the show gathered in front of their TV sets in April 2020, ready to huddle behind the sofa if things got too scary – for instance, if it was a woman. How we gazed nervously at the exhausted features of Jeremy metamorphosing teasingly into what many at first assumed to be a new work by Antony Gormley. Only time will tell how well or badly Sir Keir does but so far he has amazed us all with his gift for being able to see into the past and tell us what we should have done.

Of course, presiding over these recent tumultuous years has been the Conservative Party, or the Conservative and Unionist Party, to give it its full list of failures. Simply put, the current position that we find ourselves in, not withstanding Covid-19, can be traced back to David Cameron's promise of an EU referendum as part of his 2015 election campaign. This of course placed him in the position of having to honour his promise, which in turn placed him in the position of having to explain to the country that he was resigning, having massively fucked up.

Cameron's point, as you will remember, was that, being a keen Remainer, he was ill-starred to skipper the ship out of Europe. There was broad agreement on this and so Theresa May, another keen Remainer, was chosen to replace him. (Don't worry, nobody understood that.) May then went on a walking holiday in the

Lake District where she had a vision in which an angel told her to hold a snap election if she wanted to significantly increase her majority. And so she came back, called the election and her party was all but wiped out. Some angels are right bastards when it comes to practical jokes. Anyway, it all ended in tears at the famous Downing Street podium as it so often does, and she packed her bags and said goodbye to the circus.

As everyone knows, this is when Boris Johnson took over and so history has caught up with these pages because at the time of writing, he is still in charge. I could offer my projections on what will happen, but by now you will have realised that I like to stick to the facts rather than wildly implausible conjecture, like some writers I could name. Very soon after winning a landslide victory at the 2019 general election, Johnson pledged to deliver the country from the stranglehold of Brussels and steer the country to pastures new. True to his word, in less than a year we had secured a cracking deal with Japan, who have agreed to lift tariffs on Stilton. It's an exciting start. Were it not for Johnson's hospital stay, I am quietly confident that even more would have been achieved in his first year. Alas, it was not to be. Taking his cue from Princess Diana's noble gesture of reaching out to stigmatised HIV sufferers

' Sadly, what Diana with her two O levels understood, and Johnson with his Oxford degree didn't, was the critical variations in how different viruses transmit between hosts '

in the eighties and being seen hugging and shaking hands with them, our own Boris insisted on embracing as many Covid sufferers and carers as possible. Sadly, what Diana with her two O levels understood, and Johnson with his Oxford degree didn't, was the critical variations in how different viruses transmit between hosts. That's why she didn't go round glad-handing mucusy flu patients. And so the Prime Minister was reduced to advising us about the pandemic from the Intensive Care Unit at St Thomas's. Many have remarked that the Boris Johnson who emerged from hospital was not the same Boris Johnson who went in two weeks before. But I think we can put that down to wishful thinking. The NHS is great. But not that great.

One particular story typifies the logistical mess we were in. It is inevitable that mistakes will be made when handling a crisis as vast and wide-scale as coronavirus, and most reasonable people have been reluctant to wade in with political point-scoring at a time of universal strife. However the supply problems concerning personal protective equipment (PPE) tested us all. The stock that we had set aside for an emergency such as this was past its use-by date and so astronomical amounts of money were spent desperately trying to source replacement gear from countries that were experiencing the exact same problem. In the end, a multimillion-pound contract was hastily awarded to a Turkish T-shirt manufacturer to supply us with God knows how many 747s stuffed to the cockpit with PPE, some of which arrived suspiciously quickly. Lo and behold, much of it turned out to be Christmas-cracker quality and totally unusable. Astonishingly, ministers were actually surprised by this, which was like witnessing someone's disbelief that the handbag they bought in a market in Senegal turned out not to be genuine Gucci. Bloody outrage. They complained bitterly to the Turkish T-shirt manufacturer who by then, I assume, was shrugging his shoulders in innocence and muttering something about doing them a good deal on a villa let in Ephesus when this is all over. Despite his apparent ethical shabbiness (or maybe even because of it), I like the T-shirt guy and fondly think of him sitting at a pavement café in Istanbul, drawing on his twentieth cigarette of the morning, sipping sweet mint tea from a little glass and protesting loudly on his mobile phone to Matt Hancock, whom he constantly calls 'My friend . . .' that none of this is his fault.

Fran, I have gone on too long, like one of your boorish guests. I suppose the point I'm trying to make is that current affairs need not be taken so seriously as to cause division among friends. It boils down to this: too many people describe themselves as political when they are, in fact, ideological – unable to countenance the possibility that anyone of a view that differs even slightly from their own might have a valuable contribution to make. Such people are, by definition I would argue, usually boring, frequently delusional and sometimes very dangerous. There is absolutely nothing to gain in trying to debate, in a social setting, with an ideologue of any stripe. They already know that they are right and nothing is going to be allowed to disturb that sense of certainty, so why get involved? They belong in the same box as conspiracy theorists. A box marked 'Do Not Open'. Try gainsaying a conspiracy theorist. It provides a good example of why not to engage with people who hold rigid views. But at least conspiracy theorists have the grace to flag up their madness and that's why instinctively you wouldn't waste your time countering their arguments. If you're alert to it, you back off just about as soon as they open their stupid mouths. Because not to would mean being sucked into a vortex of mental torture, trying to talk sense to a person who has no doubt whatever that: Justin Bieber is an alien reptile; water is poisonous and that's why we all die; lockdown was a way of making us stay indoors so the government could change all the birds' batteries . . . To all these propositions, the only sensible reply is 'Sure. Bye.'

And your dinner parties are not dissimilar. Unless you are in a proper conversation that facilitates a reasonably good-natured free exchange of ideas, change the subject or get an Uber. There is no shame in turning your back on a fight in this way; on the contrary, it is a commendable strategy. Let someone else stink up the room with their haughty assertions. The worst thing you can do is to legitimise intransigent views by treating them as worthy of comment. Thank you for writing, Fran.

> *Dear Jack, Can you write my history coursework for me? It's on Chamberlain's policy of appeasement during WWII. Six thousand words should do it. Thanks!*
>
> *Carl, Bedford*

Hello Carl and thank you for reaching out to me at such a difficult time for you. I get many emails on this very subject from people in a similar situation to yours so I am well aware of the pressure that you are under. Of course I am speaking to you with my qualified psychotherapist hat on and not my comedian hat. Were it the other way round, I would already be cracking jokes about students and how late they get up etc. It is a route that every seasoned comic will instinctively choose when they discover that the cocky fellow in the front row is in fact a student. I have heard probably thousands of student put-downs over the years, but one particularly witty exchange that I was fortunate enough to witness went as follows:

> *The comedian (who shall remain nameless) on stage has struck up some banter with the punter in the front row.*
>
> COMEDIAN:
>
> What's your name?
>
> PUNTER:
>
> Er, Carl.

COMEDIAN:

And what do you do, 'Er, Carl'?

PUNTER:

I'm a student.

COMEDIAN:

A student, ladies and gentleman. Carl is a student. What do you study, Carl?

PUNTER:

History.

COMEDIAN:

History? You fucking twat.

The audience erupt in huge waves of laughter. This is a moment they will tell all their friends about. They think the comedian is a genius for coming up with a line like that, off the cuff. And it is some years before Carl ever goes back to a comedy club.

Perhaps it is because of a similar incident in your life that you now feel traumatised and no longer able to address the simple task of writing an essay on what, I imagine, is an incredibly well archived subject. After all, to my knowledge, there are at least three television channels entirely dedicated to the topic, which would suggest a decent amount of literature is available as well. Hold on, I'll check . . . Yes, just googled

'Hold on, I'll check . . . Yes, just googled 'books about WWII' and there appear to be over 87 million results, so take yer pick, I'd say'

'books about WWII' and there appear to be over 87 million results, so take yer pick, I'd say.

I used the word 'writing' but I think we both know that that is a generous description of what would be referred to, in any other circumstances, as 'cutting and pasting'. If even this seems too much of a fag, then there are websites nowadays that will, for a fee, do your coursework for you. Some people call this cheating, but really, who cares? It's only history, which is a fancy sounding word for 'what's done is done'. The books are written, the films have been made. Every possible angle has been explored in countless documentaries about the Second World War: 'Chamberlain was misunderstood'; 'Chamberlain meant well'; 'Chamberlain was a knicker-wearing, closet Nazi'. It's very possible the truth resides somewhere in between those three positions. Perhaps we shall never know. I'm just throwing in these pointers as a freebie. All you need to do now is flesh them out a little and your problem will be solved. You're very welcome, Carl.

My boyfriend seems intent on making up nicknames for our private bits and I find it hard to think of anything less sexy. I don't want to hurt his feelings – do you have any advice on how I can address it tactfully?

(Via SMS)

I have always hated nicknames, especially the one my parents gave me. 'Disappointment' hardly trips off the tongue and is four times longer than Jack anyway. In your case your boyfriend's habit of coming up with whimsical names for intimate parts of the body has become a turn-off for you. And understandably so. It must be like having sex with someone who's channelling Ken Dodd. Next time your boyfriend's parents come over, pretend to be a bit drunk and then ask them in front of him where they think he got this talent for making up nicknames from. Go into detail and tell them he calls his penis Billy Elliot and your vagina La La Land. That should stop him doing it. If he relapses, start humming show tunes and this will trigger a rightful sense of shame.

Having returned to the dating scene after a difficult divorce, I am confused as to the new protocol re paying in restaurants etc. I have met a lady that I want to ask out, but while I don't want to appear ungenerous I also don't want to offend any modern feminist-type ideas that she might have as I know how touchy that sort can be. Can you help?

Offer to pay or suggest you split the bill or wait until she offers to pay or do a runner – whatever. Just don't ever show her this letter.

> *Jack, I recently turned forty. Should I dye my hair pink and get my eyebrow pierced to distract people from my advancing years?*
>
> *Liam, Devon*

Hello Liam in Devon. It seems that you are asking *yourself* this question more than you are asking me. And that's OK. In fact it's a sign that your processing powers are still sufficiently intact to hoist the flag of doubt when your impulsive self sounds the call to action.

Whereas in parts of the world that we commonly refer to as less advanced, older people often get treated with respect, even deference, here in the West the opposite is usually the case. We see age as a sign of decrepitude, of lost faculties and shuffling to the post office in your slippers having surrendered your driving licence after that time your foot slipped on the accelerator as you were parking outside the chemist, launching your car through the shop window and into the toiletries section. Incredibly, nobody was hurt. Or even that surprised, when they realised it was you again.

No wonder some people contemplate this period of their life with such dread that they deceive themselves with the fantastic notion of somehow cranking the gears of time into reverse. Since the dawn of human existence, men have obsessed in vain with the possibilities of slowing down time, turning back time and even stopping time all together. Women, ever the more realistic, moisturised.

I won't suggest that the midlife crisis (for that is what we are discussing) is an exclusively male predicament, but my observation is that the man version is almost always more ridiculous. Some women I've spoken to who experienced this form of malaise generally addressed it in some form of self-improving and/or social activity like joining a book club, taking up yoga or doing an online degree course. Nearly always, this would have a life-affirming influence on their lives and so the potentially catastrophic crisis was effectively avoided and turned into a positive. One exception was a woman whom I shall call Laura. Although her claim of having 'gone off the rails' and 'totally lost it' in her early forties was diluted by the revelation that this wild and crazy period culminated in her having a dolphin tattooed on her left ankle.

That aside, for the men I've witnessed negotiating this hurdle, the outcome has rarely been constructive. I put this down to what I call the Wish-Fulfilment Trap©. This is dealt with in much greater detail in my book about reclaiming your masculinity, *Seize Your Manhood* (Gassling & Rimmer, 2014), which was pulped two days before the planned launch due to what was referred to in the press statement by my then publishers as 'Entirely erroneous, dangerously flawed, unscientific blah-blah-blah, we unreservedly apologise blah-blah-blah . . .' Ignore all that; that was just Trevor Gassling (who is a real cunt, by the way) venting because he had, by that point, realised that he was not going to be able to claw back a single penny of the advance thanks to my agent's brilliant if unethical addendum to the contract which, happily, had slipped through unnoticed. In fact, to give him full credit I should also state that it was a stroke of genius to submit the altered contract on the Friday afternoon of a bank holiday weekend (it's almost reassuring that you can still count on old-fashioned British laziness to that extent).

Anyway, for the purposes of this personalised response, please allow me to summarise the work: nearly all of us experience in childhood the frustration of not being able to have everything we want. This is a necessary element of parental/societal discipline that enables us to develop into properly functioning adults, instead of small-minded, vindictive sociopaths – like Trevor Gassling, for example. So far so good. The downside is that many people harbour huge resentment all through their adult lives due solely to a perceived deprivation during their youth or some minor finance-related 'fraud' (not upheld) later on in life.

Back to the Wish-Fulfilment Trap©. Let's say that as a teenager you are desperate to own a motorbike but can't afford one. That wish gets buried, you grow up, get a job, marry, have kids and life goes on. Until you suddenly realise that you are no longer young or free and that your childhood dreams have passed you by. And so emerges the sudden need to reclaim some of that youthful vim that you now lack – otherwise known as the mid-life crisis. You might not have the zest for life, the looks or the physique that you had as a youngster but you do have the money to buy that motorbike. So off you go to do just that, along with all the kit including a stupidly new-looking leather jacket. But you are

momentarily pleased with the image and vibe of it as you ride
your chrome steed down the high street, imagining that the local
teenagers are looking at you with the same awe and envy that you
felt. (In reality they don't notice you at all because they're high
on commercial adhesive.) The trouble for you starts to manifest
a week or so later when you lie awake one night and wonder why
you are not as happy or excited as you would have been had you
been able to buy the bike when you were a teenager. And then you
come to understand that the shiny Triumph on your driveway
has brought not the joy you expected, but all the frustration and
disappointment that you attached to it twenty-three years ago
when you realised you couldn't have it. Moreover, you start to
see the bike as a symbol of those lost and unrecoverable years.

You don't have to be a trained analyst like me to equate the
middle-aged desire for a motorbike in my example with your
impulse to dye your hair and stick pins through your face. It is
my guess that a sense of panic regarding your vanished youth is
overwhelming you and that your subconscious is tricking you
into thinking that a quick fix is possible. Please don't be fooled
by this. 'Crazy' hair colouring and 'wacky' body art might make
you momentarily pleased with yourself but any satisfaction soon
wears off and your eyes will betray the deep well of despair
within. If you don't believe me, just look at the people in those
BBC crowd shots of Glastonbury. Don't tell me they're not pretending. Nobody likes standing in a water-logged field with their
girlfriend on their shoulders *that* much.

And besides, and in answer to the final part of your question,
you certainly won't be distracting anyone from the reality of your

advancing years. It doesn't work like that. If you see a bus that's been graffitied, you don't think it looks like a new and better bus than all the other buses. You just think, 'Look at that crappy old bus.' If you really want to feel younger, take up a sport. At least that way you can give it up three weeks later and nobody needs to know you made a mistake.

The lady I intend to marry does not get on at all well with my daughter and is always wrongly blaming her and insisting she should either pay her way (she's 17) by doing housework etc. or move out. My loyalties are split, Jack, what should I do?

(Via SMS)

Unless your daughter has a fairy godmother, a giant pumpkin in the scullery and a host of loyal animal friends, this can only end badly. My advice to you is to learn to question the sanity of anyone who comes into your life and tries to push those who are already there out of it. There are thousands of potential dates out there for you to start again with but you only have one daughter. Ditch this cuckoo and tell her I said so if it helps.

Hi Jack. This might not seem like a massive problem but it sort of is. My friends say I shouldn't do so many favours for people at work as I already have enough on my plate. Are they right?

Sandra, Swindon

Thank you for writing, Sandra. Many problems don't seem massive but still need attention because of the damage they will cause if left unresolved and this is a classic example.

Let's face it, we all lead busy lives. On a typical day, you get up, take a shower, brush your teeth and get dressed. Maybe you have breakfast; maybe you make it for someone you live with. Maybe you have to do a sodding packed lunch for the children. You reason that it's Tuesday and decide that Tuesday can be biscuits and crisps day. But then you remember last night's TV when you watched an old episode of Louis Theroux talking to Americans who were so fat that they couldn't leave their apartments. So, you slice some carrots for them, get out the wholegrain and start spreading the low-fat cheese. Again.

Then, if you're lucky enough to be employed, you go to work. You do your work, perhaps with a break for lunch of the biscuits and crisps that you ended up taking for yourself because you were late. Then after a few more hours' work, it's the commute home.

It's your turn to cook, so on the way you stop at Tesco Express.

The walk from there is more of a struggle than it would have been if you had just paid that 5p for the carrier bag. You still don't know what stopped you. Certainly not any environmental consideration. Maybe it was an irrational attempt to disappoint the self-service checkout. Something about its turn of phrase had piqued you. 'Unidentified item . . .' Screw you, Metal Mickey. It's a fucking jar of Dolmio sauce.

You cook. You eat. You clear up. Possibly you help the kids with homework. You know less about chemistry than they do but you've watched enough *Breaking Bad* to bluff your way through. Or you help an elderly parent with an IT query. You explain that emails don't need to be printed, put into an envelope and then posted. Anyway, this reminds you to go online and pay that bill. Thank God you remembered. The last thing you need is for the Tight Budget Wine Club to withhold your next delivery.

You scan the TV channels for something interesting to watch and somehow settle for an old episode of Louis Theroux, who this time is talking to American people who married their pets. By now you're tired but you watch *Newsnight* anyway. Crime has soared and GDP has plummeted. And on that cheery note you Chubb the back door and make your way to bed.

This has been your day. You turned up at work, where, though fairly bored and frustrated, you were effective. You provided for your family. You minded your own business. You got through it.

Now relive that same day but with the addition of just one seemingly innocuous hypothetical favour which, if you bestow it, will totally balls up your life.

Let us suppose that, as you arrive at work, Mike, who has the desk opposite you, asks if you wouldn't mind swapping your turns on the rota so that you clean the kitchen 'area' today instead of tomorrow, your regular day. This, he explains, will enable him to get to an appointment with his dental hygienist. On the face of it,

not a biggy as favours go, but take a closer look and you realise that this is hugely inconvenient. You had not factored it into your diary and it will involve getting the slightly later train home. It's a much slower train – one of those that stops at every single station instead of just going to the important one, yours. Then you'll be behind on getting the dinner ready, your kids will complain that you never have time to help them with their homework,

' Admit it, you hope Mike's gums rot and he ends up with obvious and ill-fitting dentures that rattle like castanets every time he opens his mouth to ask you a favour '

that elderly relative will carry on badgering you that you still haven't sorted their email issue. As a result, you feel guilty and forget to pay the Tight Budget Wine Club, who suspend your membership. No more three-quid bottles of Romanian Chianti for you, my friend. See how your very busy but manageable daily routine has begun to unravel? And for what? So Mike can get his stupid teeth cleaned.

Plus, you realise that today is the worst day to clean the kitchen 'area' as it is the busiest day of the week in the office. You don't go as far as thinking that that was part of Mike's reason for asking this favour but as you sponge away at those tea-stained mugs and dirty soup bowls, a fleeting vignette of horror flashes across your eyes that you are not proud of. It is of Mike tripping and smashing his face on the pavement as he trots off down the road to his appointment. What a loathsome, self-centred, conniving little creep he is. Admit it, you hope Mike's gums rot and he ends up with obvious and ill-fitting dentures that rattle like castanets every time he opens his mouth to ask you a favour.

Now, just look at yourself. Standing at the sink in the kitchen 'area' at work, pent up with frustration, hatred and anger – negative, unhelpful emotional pain that you will carry with you, possibly for days. Who knows how you'll react when you see Mike with his snowy-white incisors shining through that Bee Gees perma-grin of his? Worst case scenario involves you hurling a stapler right at his face and having to be restrained on the office floor while the police are called. Only then does it dawn on you that for someone with such pristine teeth, Mike is bloody strong.

I hope that this simple example shows you, Sandra, without exaggeration or melodrama, that the issue of whether to grant favours in the workplace is not one to do with self-preservation. You are not being selfish for wanting to safeguard your carefully scheduled day from needless additional tasks imposed on you by the Mikes of this world. Your friends are right. It's time to put yourself and your needs before those of a needy colleague who cannot even organise a trip to the dentist without it severely impacting the mental health of those around him.

During lockdown, I realised that I could not spend the rest of my life with my fiancé, Warren. His controlling ways really got on my nerves and after only two and a half weeks I moved back in with my mum and stepdad. The problem is that I now feel that any new relationship should be put through a similar test before I can know if it is working, as I worry about getting involved with someone who might turn weird once we are living together. Can you suggest how I get round this?

Karen, Solihull

Thank you, Karen, for bringing this issue to me. Lockdown will be remembered for many reasons, but I suspect that top of that list will be the way in which it shone a light under the bonnet of many a relationship. It is as if you drove into the repair centre to ask about your squeaky windscreen wipers, only to be told that your car is completely unroadworthy. To further torture that metaphor, the mechanic explains that legally he can't let you get back in the car until he has fixed the problem and then scratches his head as he works out what he can rinse you for and flicks his cigarette butt, sending it rolling towards the petrol pump.

Let me put it another way. Think of yourself as blessed. Lockdown was like a microwave oven for relationships, bringing to a rapid boil issues that otherwise might have taken a lifetime of simmering before reaching that critical point of ruin. Some people take years and years to reach the moment of enlightenment that you attained after a mere fortnight. Congratulations on not wasting your life with someone who is, to use your word, weird.

Few of us enter into a relationship giving consideration to whether this is somebody we would enjoy being incarcerated with during a global pandemic. Ideally, you settle down with someone who you like waking up next to and don't dread seeing when you get home in the evening. Maybe that sounds unromantic, but let me assure you, that is a good foundation on which to build a life with somebody.

It will be helpful to take a closer look at your fiancé's behaviour so that you can get a clearer picture of what has gone wrong and how to avoid a repeat of this difficult situation. Ordinary members of the public might read your letter and simply dismiss Warren as a basket case and a total arsehole. This is understandable; however, as a professional, my job is to transcend such a layperson's approach and use politer language.

Warren, in my humble but correct opinion, is suffering from a syndrome which I first identified in a paper that I wrote last year titled 'The Uncontrolled Control Impulse© (UCI)'.* This refers to

---

* This paper was rejected by the *American Journal of Psychiatry*. I'm big enough to admit that, but utterly reject their claim that vast swathes of it were lifted, verbatim, from an earlier paper by Professor Maurice Cohen, MD, of Stanford University Medical School. The words 'wholesale' and 'plagiarism' are not what you want to see in the first line of a letter of response, but I have risen above it. It's very much their loss as far as I am concerned, and any similarity between the two papers goes to prove the adage that great minds think alike. Thank you.

a group of manipulative behaviour patterns which begin in childhood or early adulthood and which usually, though not always,
progress through the grades of seriousness as described below:

- Grade 1 is usually someone with a strong need for habit in the
  domestic setting. Typically, he/she requires the dishwasher to
  be loaded in a certain way, they are sticklers for sell-by dates
  and need to know that fresh produce is being consumed in
  order of purchase etc. Such idiosyncrasies have a sound basis
  and, while sometimes seeming to be a little bit pedantic, do
  have some value in the smooth running of a household. Very
  often this type is happier to take on domestic tasks themselves
  rather than stand back and witness them being done 'incor-
  rectly'. As a matter of fact, my advice is, if you find yourself
  living with someone like this: sit back and enjoy. You can
  legitimately say, 'I tried to help but you didn't want it done
  how I was doing it and frankly, I'm not going to hoover the
  flat in a specific direction because if I do, according to you, the
  carpet will last longer (I've googled it; it's not even a thing).
  So from now on, I'll read the paper and drink coffee while
  you vacuum, even if it means that some people will assume
  that I am just a lazy prick.' But before you begin to worry that
  you have missed out on the opportunity to have a free house
  servant for life, read on, because my belief is that Warren's
  issues suggest a more serious case of UCI.
- Grade 2. This is the less mild version of Grade 1 and where
  I think your ex resides. Not only do tasks have to be done in
  a certain way, but also in a certain order. Failure to comply

with these stipulations might incur some equally fictional karmic retribution. A standard example of this might be, 'If I don't clean all the white tiles in the bathroom before the blue ones, then the rest of my day will be bad, because my house will catch fire.' It is exhausting to live under the governance of such a messed-up concept of cause and effect. I suggested to one sufferer that he call as many fire stations as he can and ask if they have ever known a house fire to start like this. My thinking was that repeated conversations with different experts in the field would help him build a picture of how unlikely his theory was. However, what happened is that my client switched his obsession from how to clean tiles to calling no fewer and no more than forty-three (God only knows why it was forty-three, what a fruitcake) fire stations every single day. Naturally, the forfeit for failing to reach this magic number was that his bathroom tiles would all simultaneously crack and fall off the wall – something that would actually need a Hollywood special effects department to make happen.

- Grade 3. You've guessed it, Grade 3 is often a worsened state of Grade 2. Every action has a consequence. Wash your car from back to front instead of the other way round or you will crash and burn next time you drive it. Use an odd number of teabags during the day and you'll die in your sleep that night. Never go into buildings that have yellow doors, and so on. Very distressing for the sufferer but unbearable for a cohabitant who is being forced to obey these nonsensical edicts.

- Grade 4. Don't even go there. This is where coercive tendencies go unchecked for so long that they metastasise into a full-blown 'It puts the lotion on the skin' and 'Everyone line up and get your cyanide drink' type of thing. In fairness, such people are few and far between, at least the ones who make the headlines are. Nobody really has reliable data on it, presumably because control freaks at this level are hard to pin down and get to fill out the relevant forms and surveys. And let's face it, who wants to hand a person like that something as sharp as a Bic? I mean, come on. Besides, Charles Manson was notoriously slack when it came to paperwork, although this is not a well-known fact, probably because it is somewhat eclipsed by his other shortcomings.

• There is a Grade 5 but I don't think we need to explore that deeply upsetting mental landscape today. Suffice it to say, Grade 5 is reserved for international terrorists, war criminals and a certain deceased *Top of the Pops* presenter from the 1970s. Unless there is something you have not told me about Warren, I feel we can move on, satisfied with my diagnosis that he is a Grade 2 UCI type.

Understandably, you have asked me how you might put future relationships through a similar test so that you can avoid getting seriously involved with a similarly screwed-up character. It is a sensible question, Karen, and one which I will now try to answer.

Let's assume that the ghastliness of the pandemic has receded and that normal rules of life have been more or less re-established. So, you meet someone who, on first impression, you find agreeable, you go on a couple of dates and things are going well. Let's call him Andy. Andy comes across to you as a really nice guy. But then, so did Warren at first. Naturally, you are anxious not to make the same mistake twice. I think that there are a series of relatively simple steps you can take to discover whether Andy is a potential nightmare or not. Here is a strategy for you. It comprises a series of tests that you can set without him even knowing.

Suppose that, on your second or third date, Andy compliments you on your outfit. Next time you meet, wear something completely different in style and see if he mentions it. If he says how nice you look, then fine, that would suggest that he's into you as a person, which is what you want. But if he blurts out, 'I preferred it when you wore the tight-fit jeans with the silky red halter neck from Zara,' then alarm bells should ring. Quite apart from being plain rude, and overlooking the highly unsettling amount of detail in his description, that statement should make you run a mile, tight-fit jeans or not. Because what is truly disturbing about Andy and the real cause for concern is that he has basically requested, in a sly way, that next time you wear what he wants you to wear. This is unacceptable, as I'm sure you will recognise. It is possible that you could call him out at this stage and tell him you don't appreciate his comments but you have to ask yourself: is that likely to change his ways? And, secondly, do I really want to be providing cognitive behavioural therapy on what is supposed to be a trip to the cinema? If the answer to either of these questions is 'no', then it would seem sensible to nip the relationship in the bud and start over with someone else. Otherwise, you're looking at investing a great deal of time and emotional energy in somebody who secretly fetishises you as a mannequin on which he can drape all his favourite women's clothes. Stuff like that happens all the time and you could go for years not realising until one day you come home and find Andy unconscious with his head in your laundry basket.

But hopefully he will pass this first and most basic test and you can take things further. Now, what you should do is if, say, he suggests meeting on Friday night, tell him that you can't do that as you are going out with your girlfriends, but how about Saturday? What you want from this is simply for Andy to say, 'Great, have fun on Friday and I'll look forward to seeing you on Saturday.' Then you want Saturday to be a fun date without being asked where you went, who you saw, were there any guys there, what did you wear, why did you wear the halter neck from Zara if I wasn't there? Who did you sleep with? What were their names? Etc. etc. etc. Now you know that Andy belongs to the most tedious group of people on earth. He is a pathologically jealous, needy man-baby and you don't want a sicko like that in your life. Before long he'll be demanding to know

> **Before long he'll be demanding to know your iPhone password and locking all your shoes in a cupboard whenever he goes out**

your iPhone password and locking all your shoes in a cupboard whenever he goes out. He almost certainly won't change; like a rescue pit bull who seems cute for the first few weeks, and then one morning when you unwittingly pick up a broom – the chosen weapon of his previous, cruel owner – he can't help himself, lunging and sinking his teeth into your neck.

Karen, this is your potential that Andy is consuming. Reclaim it before you look in the mirror and see your older self, weary and worn down by an infantile, foot-stamping emotional bully who you tolerated at first and who repaid you with a life sentence of haranguing, nagging, coercion and sulky insistence on getting his own way. Andy's a tosser. Deal with it. Then you are ready to try again. And again, if need be, until you find the right guy who is undemanding in all of the ways mentioned above. You are in a minority in that you can be thankful for Covid-19 and the restrictions it imposed on us. As they say, it's an ill wind that blows no good and on this occasion it filled your sails and took you to a better place.

Ten months ago, I borrowed £2500 from a friend to start a small business. The deal was that I would pay him back after a year plus 2.5 per cent interest. However, he has now produced the agreement which I signed but it is clear to me that he has doctored it to lose the decimal point and is claiming I owe him 25 per cent instead. I obviously would never have agreed to this and am kicking myself that I didn't ask for my own copy but he is being dead serious that I should pay him this massive interest. What should I do?

(Via SMS)

This really depends how hard you are.

Very hard: Stare him in the face and say in a soft voice you are disappointed. Done well, this will send a deathly chill through him and he'll ask your forgiveness and tell you to forget about the interest and, for that matter, the loan.

Quite hard: Tell him that was a funny joke, here's what we agreed and if he wants any more he can whistle for it.

Not at all hard: Pay him all the money back plus the 25 per cent interest and spend the rest of your life plotting a revenge that you know you don't have the courage to carry out.

Not at all hard as such but mentally unstable: Hire someone who *is* very hard to stare him in the face and say in a soft voice how disappointed you are etc. etc.

Dear Jack, What is your view on manbags? I am worried about looking stupid if I use one, but on the other hand find it hard to fit everything into my pockets without causing unsightly bulges.

Paul, Chislehurst

OK Paul, it might be useful first if we define some terms as I feel this will help you to see how specific your anxiety actually is.

What I mean by a manbag is a (usually) leather wallet-like case no larger than a sheet of A4 paper and generally a bit smaller. It may have a zip or even close with a buckle at the front and will very often have a small strap to slip your hand through so that it can dangle, though I hasten to add that, even if you take the brave step of getting one, swinging your bag is not advised for reasons that cannot be given without risking accusations of hate speech.

Before I go any further, however, I need to own up to a historic admiration of the type of bag just described. By historic I mean the 1970s when I first went on family holidays and exchange trips to France. This was when, as an impressionable boy, I first encountered the phenomenon that we are discussing. In those days, no adult male Frenchman was seen without his well-worn leather companion. There was never a murmur that this was in any way effeminate (and let's be clear, that is one of the main hetero fears attached to owning such an accessory). Your Frenchman would carry it everywhere, as if it were an extension of his arm, and it invariably contained a crumpled blue pack of filterless Gauloises, a Bic lighter and keys to his probably unroadworthy 2CV. As if any perceived effeminacy of the wrist tote was more than offset by its potentially life-threatening contents. Anyway, aged eleven, I thought these bags were really cool, not least because they further accessorised smoking, a hobby that I had already resolved to take up properly as soon as I could afford to.

But somehow, no Brit ever truly got away with using one of these bags; not in Britain anyway. Oh, lots tried, of course. For many misguided Britons, the handy clutch became a holiday purchase, boldly brought out and used back home, gripped self-consciously on trial outings to the corner shop to pay the paper bill. Perhaps buoyed by the apparent obliviousness of the newsagent, a second more audacious trip to the garden centre would be planned and executed without incident. But then on the third sortie (this time the big one), to the pub, the brave holder is instantly greeted with, 'Oooh, get you! Like your handbag, ducky,' from the girl behind the bar. This prompts howls of laughter from all the customers and the returned holidaymaker's unspoken resolution to ditch the damn thing and never be seen with it again.

Throughout the seventies, scenes like these were played out all over Britain. Some persevered for longer, but eventually all the little leather imports were decommissioned. There was certainly no demand for them on the second-hand market. And so it is that most attics in the United Kingdom that have not been cleared out from that era house an abandoned holiday manbag.

Coming back to present-day Britain, there still exists a demand for an acceptable, non-stupid male version of the handbag. However, the question remains: how does a fellow carry his essentials around without appearing to have borrowed something from a lady's wardrobe? A solution is still needed if he is to avoid the unfortunate-looking pocket bulges that you allude to.

So I will now list some other types of (what could be described as) manbag, along with my views on them, so that you can hopefully make the right decision for yourself.

The backpack is now pretty much ubiquitous and is arguably the best solution. But, while it has great advantages, such as being unisex, comfortable and purpose made, there are a few problems that I would draw your attention to.

If you go for an expensive high-tech model, i.e. one that is really designed for serious trekking cross-country, or even mountaineering, it can give the impression of someone who considers his environment to be hostile, even threatening, and therefore requiring nothing less than state-of-the-art survival gear. It's no coincidence that those unfortunate souls who turn up for Extinction Rebellion rallies all feel the need to wear them. I know they have mostly journeyed in from the Home Counties and you can't always get a seat on the busier lines, and yes, that houmous snack pack isn't going to carry itself, but emergency-grade equipment projects a paranoia that is not warranted on the average stroll up Park Lane. Even if you *are* worried about the climate.

Secondly, if you wear a suit *and* a backpack you generally look like a dysmorphic schoolboy who's just skived off PE. When it comes to style, mixing genres can work to your advantage, but not in this case. The Austin Reed/North Face combo is a no-no.

And it can't be solved by investing in an executive version, which is basically a dad joke that you wear. Don't ask me how I know. And if you go to work in a suit, get a briefcase like a proper grown-up or change jobs so you can dress down and get away with looking like an Alpine guide.

The sling is a mutant of the backpack. It is really a single-strapped backpack that you wear across the body and has the advantage of being easier to put on. But there is always a downside, isn't there? And the downside of the sling is that it instantly turns you into a dick, which is why it hasn't really taken off and why you must never get one.

Then there is the messenger bag – by far the best and most practical solution. That is, if you are a messenger. If you are not, then you should stay well clear. Cyclists are excused in this case as, for them, the messenger is an ideal bag and because style is so patently not a concern for them anyway.

Next on the list is what is termed by the luggage cognoscenti as a 'crossover'. This is the direct descendent of the manbag but with a long enough strap for it to hang across the body. Unless you are a male model on a catwalk or a member of the St John Ambulance Brigade, then you have no business owning one.

The bumbag, which is a sort of sporran that's had chemotherapy, is inexcusable and yet remains very popular, especially with Americans and old people. I'm happy to give a free pass to our senior citizens; if you can't stick two fingers up at couture in your dotage, then when can you? Americans, however, cannot be pardoned in the same way. I am sure that we all very much enjoy welcoming tourists to this country but I for one find it upsetting to have to see them waddling around with so little dignity. Unless you are now entering old age and are so forgetful that you have to strap everything that's important (warfarin, Murray Mints, endless small change etc.) to your waist, the bumbag is not for you, Paul.

Some people opt for the carrier bag and there are arguments that support this being a good idea. It is commonly thought to be a mugging deterrent because assailants do not associate Asda or Sainsbury's with nickable assets (unless they are actually in Asda or Sainsbury's, in which case they help themselves to as many assets as they can stuff down their trousers). One friend I could mention chooses the carrier bag for his belongings whenever he is going to the pub after work because he knows that, left behind in a drunken haze, a crumpled bag of incomprehensible notes, biros and betting slips is less likely to trigger a bomb scare than his usual briefcase. In a funny sort of way it is actually quite thoughtful of him, but not an example that normal drinkers need to worry about following.

Perhaps the most eccentric solution that I am aware of is the gilet. The type of thin, sleeveless jacket covered in multiple pockets and zippers favoured by anglers. I expect they are handy when fishing but no man needs to turn himself into a walking desk tidy for the sake of somewhere to keep a bunch of keys.

Perhaps by now, Paul, you have given up on your quest but please don't be disheartened. Whether or not to acquire a manbag is a very serious matter and I have treated it as such. It was important that I outline these few simple rules for you to be able to confidently find your way forward and choose the right option for you. I hope that helps. And remember, if you do press the nuclear button and go for it, stay away from your local. Like, forever.

I'm 27 and I'm still a virgin. It's now become such a big issue that I'm scared of getting into a relationship because I'm embarrassed to tell people and nervous about doing the wrong thing. It's really affecting my confidence. Help!

(Via SMS)

For thousands of years virginity was revered as a sacred status but now it's seen as strange, sad or just a natural side effect of playing Warhammer. When you do get into a relationship, confide that your fantasy is that you're a virgin and like being shown what to do. Hopefully they'll go along with it and you will have a perfect alibi for your first experience. It's worth noting that the possible negative is they will see this as a cue to divulge *their* fantasy. The feedback I've had from another client with a similar predicament is that if this does happen, you should argue that the two fantasies are non-compatible and leave. You really don't want your first experience forever marred by having to play a traffic warden with a particularly unkind way of issuing tickets.

> *Dear Jack, one of my oldest friends is getting married and wants to have his stag do in Vegas. I just can't afford it and even if I could I'm not sure that's how I want to spend my money. He's pissed off with me. Any advice on what to do?*
>
> *Rick, Plymouth*

Part of me wants you to go, Rick. Find the money somehow and get to Vegas. The chance won't come again to see your friend hit the town high on fentanyl bought from the slick hotel concierge ('Have a nice day, sir') and blow his house deposit on a card game he doesn't know the name of, much less understand. However, I do acknowledge that that is a part of me of which I am not hugely proud. One obvious solution that these difficult times offer is to say that you have bought a ticket, then on the day pull out due to a high temperature, dry cough and sudden loss of taste. (Maybe throw in chronic diarrhoea – not really a symptom of Covid-19, but a sufficiently scary thought to put anyone off having you come along. Nobody partying needs a panicky bog-sprinter killing the vibe.)

This strategy could certainly work, but let's look at what will happen if you skip the stag do then attend the subsequent nuptials. The last thing we want is for you to get to the wedding only to find that you've been ostracised, left out on the big day like Meghan Markle's dad, relegated in your peer group; that you're not on the table with your mates, as you expected, having a laugh, but stuck at the back of the hall, near the door to the kitchen, in between the groom's nan and great-nanna. The catering staff will assume you just want tea on your table and you'll spend the worst two hours of your life having to agree with your companions on a whole range of topics that you'd never previously given any thought to but which all somehow boil down to immigration. 'Agree' because to engage in a meaningful exchange of views would require levels of commitment, not to mention diction and volume, that would daunt even an experienced care worker. So you sit through the meal nodding and yessing to every random thought they utter. Finally, it's time for the speeches and because nan and great-nanna even now won't bloody shut up you extract yourself and stand by the bar. The best man gets a huge round of applause for his American tales of derring-do. Is it just you being paranoid, or was there a tone of exclusion you detected in all those references to Las Vegas?

Later, as the dancing starts underneath the glitter ball, you grab another beer and join your mates, chirpily asking, 'How was it, then? Vegas?' Best to grab the bull by the horns, so to speak. But their taciturn shrugs and 'Yeah, good' replies leave you squirming like an impaled matador. An attempted explanation for your party-pooping is greeted with a too-eager acceptance that seems to kill the subject dead. Except a few minutes later, as you sup on your bottle of Beck's, one of the Vegas lads (because that's what they are calling themselves now), Naz, speaks into your ear. The music has become incrementally louder so that all you can make out from Naz is something about being 'out of order' and 'stag do'. He turns his back, raises his arms in a drunken roar and joins the others who roar back at him. And now Whitney Houston wants to dance with somebody but, knowing your luck, not you.

Like I said, Rick, that's the last thing we want for you and my job is to help you to navigate your way through this problem. The golden rule with a situation such as this is not to blow it up in your mind into an imagined scenario in which everything has gone wrong. That is called projection and it is an unhealthy way to think.

The stag party has changed dramatically over the years and, many would argue, not for the better. My own stag was a thoroughly enjoyable affair involving a few martinis at a club I belong to in Dean Street, followed by dinner at an excellent restaurant with plenty of good wine, champagne and probably one too many brandies. The fact that I chose not to invite anybody to join me was remarked upon at the time as 'eccentric', but to each his own. Some enjoy company; I enjoy a crossword. My reasoning at the time was that there would be plenty of people allowed to the wedding; why should I let them spoil my big night as well?

The modern stag, as you have discovered with your friend's arrangements, has become a drawn-out affair that is rarely shorter than a weekend and often as long as fourteen days if you include time spent in custody. Similarly, hen nights are a very regular feature of any town centre with a nightclub. Hen night participants are easier to identify; one clue is they wear sashes that say 'HEN NIGHT'. Another is that they carry giant inflatable penises around with them and try to get off with the paramedics who are holding their hair for them while they vomit.

' Some enjoy company; I enjoy a crossword '

It would be easy to look upon these people with scorn but that would be a mistake. They are merely acting out their interpretation of a ritual. All around the world, forthcoming marriages are celebrated in diverse ways according to the country, region or even village. These may involve anything from plate-smashing (Germany) to shooting arrows at the bride (China – spoiler alert, she isn't hurt). Plus everything in between: the tribal dances, the singing, the communal crying for a month before the wedding. Incidentally, the crying thing is China as well. Admittedly, it's not entirely unfeasible that the shooting tradition could have gone badly wrong which led to the crying tradition.

As wildly different as all these customs and ceremonies are, they share one important feature: community. Whenever I see a documentary about remote villages in distant countries featuring locals in their magnificent costumes and full headgear acting out a ceremonial dance – whether it be to invoke rain, declare hostilities, mark a forthcoming marriage or maximise income from gullible film crews and tourists – I find the total involvement of all the community one of the most impressive elements. There is something very moving about it, as though the ritual binds everybody to a common hope. For me, it's impossible to imagine anybody in one of those villages going to the elder and asking to be excused because they've got a bad back or the football's on or, worst of all, they're 'not sure that's how they want to spend their money'. The single, primary purpose of these events is to unify groups of people in a shared endeavour.

And that brings me to you, Rick. It brings me to the point where I have to ask you to re-examine the role you wish to play in your friend's life. I understand and sympathise with your financial issue but am concerned about your stated unwillingness to get involved in your mate's stag do even if you could afford it. It suggests a comradely impulse that you have long stopped listening to. You have two alternatives: (1) find yourself at the wedding, in circumstances I have already described with pinpoint accuracy, i.e. slowly coming to terms with ostracism; or (2) walk away from the friendship now and start again somewhere else.

The latter is extreme but more common than you'd think. Take comfort from the fact that your social exclusion will at least be semi-voluntary. You can walk away from everybody in your circle with head held high, knowing it is for the better and saddened only by the grating silence of nobody saying you should stay. Be grateful you are allowed to break ranks without censure. In some tribal settings it is customary for dissidents, apostates and people who can't be bothered to hunt their own food to be driven from the village in a grim fanfare of caterwauling and turd-throwing. Hence the unlucky reject is consigned to a scary existence of nomadic foraging and sleeping rough, like Bear Grylls but with no one to show off to. It all sounds a bit harsh, but to be fair, it's not easy to exclude someone any other way in a settlement of nine huts and a well. Admittedly, I have never personally travelled to any such place in my life but I have read enough back copies of *National Geographic* to know exactly what I'm talking about, which in many ways is better than travelling as you don't need the jabs.

So there you have it, Rick. I'm afraid it boils down to a 'join in or get lost' choice. Hopefully I have helped you to step back and examine the bigger picture using my extensive knowledge of anthropology. It's not the approach most therapists would take, but then again, I am not most therapists.

During lockdown my girlfriend cut my hair and wants to continue doing it, even though I can now go out and get it done properly. She reckons she did a great job and that it saves money and she was offended when I said I'd rather go to a barber. What should I do?

This is a classic case of double standards and can lead to great resentment further down the line if left unchecked. Explain that if it's about saving money then surely you should both be doing this and that you should therefore be cutting hers. Then explain that you intend to post the hilarious results on social media to raise money for charity. I think she'll back down.

The woman I want to marry is 23 years younger than me. I know this has raised a few eyebrows amongst my friends and hers, and her parents are very wary of me, but we love each other. I assume people must think she's after my money or that any children we are lucky enough to have might end up fatherless. Am I being naive about this? Is it doomed from the outset?

(Via SMS)

The rules for this type of carry-on are clearly set out in a paper which I recently submitted to the Official British Council of Psychotherapy. I am yet to hear back from them but can tell you that my suggested guidelines on relationship age gaps in which the male is older are as follows:

18/41 = **creepy**
28/51 = **not exactly creepy but still wrong**
38/61 = **whatever**
48/71 = **the dirty old bugger**
58/81 = **that poor woman.**

Think of this not as a judgement but as a guide – a tool for life, which evidently is how her family think of you.

Hello Leonard. I am glad that you have asked for guidance before taking any further measures on your own. Reading your question for the first time I experienced a nano moment of suspense when you described offering to tidy Brian and Siobhan's garden for them. It is not unknown for such encounters to escalate and become a headline on the local news. You think their front lawn is a mess now, but imagine it with a police tent and five or six SOCOs in forensic suits taking it in turn to be sick from what they've seen. And the journalist, desperately trying to conceal her glee at not just reporting another stolen mobility scooter: 'The victim is known as Leonard Simpson and was found with a trowel that had been pushed up his arse shortly after tea-time . . . A neighbour, who didn't wish to be named, said that Mr Simpson was a quiet man who would do anything to help his neighbours . . .'

So, first up, Leonard, please read Brian's aggression as a sign to back the hell off. Your claim that your neighbourhood is 'nice' does not match the reality of what you have described and it is time for you to face facts. A friendly and helpful gesture on your behalf was treated as an imposition and triggered a hostile response from Brian, which, as I have already illustrated, could have been so very much worse.

And what of Siobhan? The quiet one in the pack? It is rare that a spouse is completely unaware of their partner's darker side. She will have heard the commotion on her doorstep when it all kicked off. Did she intervene? No. Did she join Brian in telling you to 'F*** off, you tosser' (which is what I am guessing he said)? No, she didn't do that either. I have to ask myself why that would be. And one very viable explanation is that she is the brains in that partnership and Brian is the brawn. Siobhan will have stayed in her armchair, happy in the knowledge that mutton-headed Brian would handle the situation with all the subtlety of a scaffolder who has been asked if he could possibly work more quietly.*

At the risk of sounding like I am exaggerating, I would say that number 4 is a tinder box of violence and that it is quite possible that you have a Fred and Rosemary West situation brewing beneath your nose. Think what that could do to house prices in your street. When it all comes out and they discover the tumble dryer is actually a grim headstone and Brian and Siobhan get taken away with blankets over their heads, then how will you feel? Their front door and windows will have to be boarded up to stop yobs breaking into the 'House of Horrors' for dares. The council might even bulldoze it – after all, who'd want to live there? And then you can forget all about your Best-Kept Residential Street awards. The most you could hope for then would be a mention in one of those 'Haunted England' guide books. You'll get tourists taking selfies and wondering out loud how anyone could live in such a creepy road. House by house, your neighbours will move in the hope of finding a happier place to live. Their gardens then will also become neglected and dishevelled until the whole street looks like a giant compost heap,

> **I would say that number 4 is a tinder box of violence and that it is quite possible that you have a Fred and Rosemary West situation brewing beneath your nose**

* Full disclosure: I know this because I actually did ask a scaffolder that exact question one hot day last summer. It is this experience that informed my guess as to what Brian said to you.

but with chimneys. Except for your house, of course. You'll keep the flag flying for what was once a decent area, but it won't be the same. People will talk of Leonard, the strange old guy who still lives in Brian and Siobhan's street and still mows his front garden even though all the other gardens are covered in old appliances, syringes and used johnnies.

I think most readers will agree that, so far, what I have presented is well thought through and entirely reasonable, but for the sake of balance I will suggest a different assessment. It's something of a long shot, I know, but suppose Brian and Siobhan are just not much into gardening. Not everyone relishes the prospect of spending all day creating needless toil for themselves by trying to maintain a pristine lawn and borders. As the French would say: *chacun à son goût*, which, roughly translated, means 'everyone gets gout'.

Leonard, you are one of those lucky people who derive great joy from making your garden as picturesque as possible. But there are others – and perhaps your neighbours at number 4 are like this – who simply hate everything (and everyone, it would seem) connected with horticulture. I myself have experienced moments of despair in the pursuit of green perfection. Without wishing to sound too esoteric, all gardens break down into two types of plants: weeds and stuff you paid for. And gardening is the unending battle of trying to defend the latter from the former. It is futile and, in the end, I gave up. Gardening is a war against nature and I have become a conscientious objector.

Or, put another way, most hobbies are input-dependent, i.e. they progress in direct proportion to your effort. For example, say you decided to build a model of the Eiffel Tower out of matches: you would know that every time you returned to the project, ready to continue the build, you would find it exactly as you left it. This is true even if you took a break from your modelling for several months. Well, gardening is the exact opposite: take even a short holiday and you will return to something that bears no resemblance to what you left. Thistles will be standing tall as toilet brushes all over your lawn and bindweed will have slid its strangling limbs around all your favourite shrubs. In other words, gardening is a hobby that sabotages itself. Carry on with your delusion as much as you like but a garden's true allegiance is not to us and our feeble secateurs but to Mother Nature herself.

It could be, then, could it not, that Brian has found himself in my situation. He gave gardening a go, found it satisfactory for a short while, and then gardening had a go back at him and he realised he didn't want a hobby that knows how to retaliate. He knows that to let you and your well-meaning chums do a *Ground Force* number would be suicide. Yes, his garden would look nice for a week or so, but the consequences would be unthinkable and could even result in him conceding his front path to a flash mob of giant stinging nettles hell-bent on a revenge land grab.

This is the bit you never see on those make-over shows: What happens once the busybodies who do your place up leave. The camera crew have done their job. They hovered around while the owners are led in, blindfolded. Then the big reveal. They got the money shot: those close-ups of them getting all teary and saying they could never have done all this themselves. (At which point I always think, 'Obviously not. That's why you rang the television programme, isn't it? And haven't you done well out of it? Free decking, an ornamental pond, brand-new shed and a pagoda. You jammy bastards, I'd be crying.') And that's a wrap. Thank you very much. Join us next week when we'll be transforming somebody else's dump into a gauche, geranium-filled gimmick-fest. Goodbye. And the poor unsuspecting sods are left with a show garden that will, over the course of a few short weeks, morph itself into an unusable cemetery of wilting flowers and dead goldfish.

And so it is that Brian finds himself assaulted on all fronts. By the mission-creeping vegetation; by Siobhan, who never misses an opportunity to belittle him; and now by you and your cohorts, pressuring him into a course of action that he instinctively knows would be utter madness. I know you meant well, Leonard, but that is not enough in itself to qualify your cause as just. I say this: unless you are prepared to revamp his garden and then maintain it in perfect condition in perpetuity, at no cost to Brian, then leave the poor man and his wife alone.

> *I've just been dumped by text. We've been seeing each other for six months now and while there wasn't any talk of moving in together or the like, I definitely felt like the relationship was going somewhere and I'm sure we had fun together. Where did things go wrong?*
>
> (Via SMS)

Things went wrong when you met a sociopath. Trust me, you're better off without him/her.

Dear Jack, I secretly hate my husband's parents. How do I deter them from visiting at Christmas?

Maggie, Leeds

Hello Maggie. I first want to address one particular detail that you raise: Christmas. Perhaps the greatest irony of Christianity is that to celebrate its founder's birth we spend anything up to a week wishing various members of our extended family would slip on some black ice and fall under a passing skip lorry. This is a difficult admission to make and you have been brave to come forward with it.

One of the sources of your unhappiness is the shame that surrounds the subject. For some reason it is still frowned upon to simply pour a couple of glasses of wine one evening in November and say to our partner, 'I've been thinking and the fact is I'd rather take a stick blender to my private parts than have your tedious, judgemental bloody parents for Christmas. Is that OK with you?' To which, he or she, if they are reasonable, would most likely reply. 'Fair enough, I'll text them now. We'll just have a quiet one this year. Top up?'

Domestic tension is a theme that is strikingly absent in Christmas merchandise. I imagine this is because none of us really wants an Advent calendar with little windows that open each day to depict a new scene of family strife. Most of us are quite content with pictures of angels and kings, knowing that the full horror of the day will reveal itself in due course. As a matter of fact, a few years ago I made a pitch to one of the big card manufacturers with my idea for a post-Advent calendar which had windows to open throughout January, each one showing a little vignette from my take of what would have happened in the anticlimactic period following the birth of baby Jesus. Thus we'd see Mary having a go at Joseph for his rubbish hotel-booking skills or arranging to take back the myrrh and frankincense and swap it for something useful like a pram. As the month continued, you'd have Joseph saying exactly what he thought of the innkeeper on Tripadvisor or trading the donkey in for an estate car. Sadly, I had the misfortune to speak with the CEO of the card company whose lack of vision was matched only by her inability to articulate her opinion using inoffensive language.

Maybe one day this country will breed a generation of business leaders whose talents will include being able to spot raw creativity in the likes of me, but until then we are probably better off in the annual state of amnesia that allows us to believe that this Christmas things will somehow be different. At least we can enjoy the build-up to it even if the actual day is a waking nightmare.

And yet it would be a mistake to think of ourselves as being without agency in the matter. You explain in your letter that you 'secretly hate' your in-laws and wish to deter them from coming for Christmas. With another correspondent in this book

I explained the method of 'shunning' as a way of slowly and surreptitiously diminishing the target's sense of ease to the extent that they eventually retreat completely from your life. This might be of use to you but my instinct is that you will not have time to grind these two visitors down in time for the festive season. So I am going to recommend another technique, which I call 'reverse shunning'.

The name itself will have given you quite a clue, but I will elaborate. Whereas in 'shunning' we purposely and meticulously dismantle the framework of somebody's *raison d'être* in the hope of triggering an existential crisis, in 'reverse shunning' we achieve the same end but with a directly opposite approach.

Begin by overstating, as shrilly as you can, how welcome they are to stay as long as they would like to and declaring that you are beside yourself with excitement. This tone will be baffling and cause them to wonder whether you are now certifiably bipolar and currently experiencing an extreme high that is likely to be followed by a similarly alarming low – one that might even reach its nadir of bleak, howling angst on Christmas morning itself. All of a sudden they start to feel their stay with you is less of a great idea and yet all you have done is said how thrilled you are that they are coming. If your husband is on board, get him to confide that he is worried about you and the less excitement you have, the better it will be for everyone concerned.

When they ask if they can bring anything (all in-laws ask this but never mean it), chirpily rattle through a detailed list which includes a 9-kilo Norfolk Bronze organic turkey and all the booze.* Jokily add that it's only fair as you'll be paying for the cocaine, but say it in such a manic voice that it sounds as though you actually already have. Then perhaps add that you are shipping the kids off to their other grandparents for the duration so that 'We can get on with having a proper bender.' Again, say it as a joke, but one that might conceivably not really be a joke at all.

Without prompting, continue by telling them what you'd love for Christmas is a new flat-screen and, without pausing for breath, reel off the details of the new 70-inch Samsung and that this is so incredibly kind of them and that you feel like crying as you never thought you'd own such a lovely telly until they asked.

This way, you are gently pushing them away while appearing to be pulling them into your embrace. Almost without fail, this method results in a phone call two or three days later from the same in-laws to say that they feel awkward but have been invited to spend Christmas on a 'caravan trip of a lifetime with some old

> **Jokily add that it's only fair as you'll be paying for the cocaine, but say it in such a manic voice that it sounds as though you actually already have**

---

* I suggest that you be quite specific on this as well. Don't leave it to them, the old tightwads, or you'll end up drinking Morrisons' paint thinner, or worse still, Morrisons' wine. Casually demand certain growers and vintages, spirits for cocktails and plenty to go round too, in case next door drop in. (By the way, I have plenty of tips to stop that happening as well.)

friends, touring the West Midlands' and very much didn't want to miss out on the opportunity. All that remains is for you to be magnanimously understanding and acknowledge that of course you will miss them but will try to have a nice time without them.

> *I'm coming up to the end of my second year of uni and I have done nothing, almost literally nothing. I have pretended to my friends, family and housemates that I go off to lectures but secretly go back to bed or sit in the park. I've fallen so far behind now that I don't know what to do. I'm trapped in my lie. What should I do?*
>
> *(Via SMS)*

Learn from this experience and embrace it as who you are: someone who bucks the system and isn't afraid to stick two fingers up at the rules. Hold your head up high and know that the world is a big place and somewhere out there is a dead-end job waiting for you.

Dear Jack, I've recently grown a beard and it is a different colour to the hair on my head: my hair colour is dark brown and my beard is ginger. Should I dye my beard brown or my hair ginger? Or is the contrast attractive/acceptable?

Byron, Stoke Newington

Hi Byron, or perhaps I should say 'Yo'. I'm excited because I have never met or much less corresponded with anybody called Byron. The fact that you also live in that hub of hipsterism known as Stoke Newington *and* have now grown a beard (I'll come to that in a bit) tells me that you are clearly fully committed to an enviable lifestyle of modern urban coolness. Not all who try succeed in becoming a hipster and I am frequently asked for advice on how to make the transition, even though I myself have never felt called to the cheesecloth.

During the day, hipsters, both male and female, can most commonly be seen coasting past on old-fashioned bicycles, looking for all the world like extras from a movie about the Dutch resistance. In fact, they will be purposefully travelling between appointments – hipsters are famously entrepreneurial and have been known to have several start-ups on the go at one time. Projects that I have known of include a small company that made bespoke ukuleles out of recycled Monopoly boards. They didn't actually sell well (beyond the performance-poetry circuit where two were purchased by a double act who subsequently had to flog them on Gumtree, ironically due to rent arrears). But that is less important, claims their website, than 'the fact that the instruments exist and are cherished by their owners'. Amazing.

Another example was the Real Tipi Company. Wonderful, authentic tents made from actual buffalo hide. Sadly, an initial burst of popularity was followed by a rapid abandonment of the design due to accusations of cultural appropriation from a small but aggressive folk music group called Running Water who claimed to have Native American heritage and were offended by the exploitation of their people's traditional camping skills. Matters were not improved when the animal rights lot waded in. The founder of the Real Tipi Company had little choice but to borrow even more money from his parents and launch a vegan version of the tent. However, the papyrus he used was not well researched and proved to be a grave fire hazard that practically dissolved in light rain.

Running Water themselves fell on their sword some months later when they released an EP that sampled some Mongolian throat singing. This also was deemed to be cultural appropriation by various activists. The group's lead singer received death threats from a woman called Sandra, a self-styled social justice warrior. Sandra worked as a fairness liaison officer for Haringey Council, but in her spare time liked to tell people she disagreed with that she was going to kill them. Anyway, she got a two-month suspended sentence for her troubles but kept her job, which is nice.

When hipsters aren't running businesses, you can see them

in artisan coffee shops comparing notes on the new oat-milk macchiato or just listening contentedly on headphones to Tame Impala.

It's a common misconception that being a hipster means eschewing consumerism; however, this is not the case. What is true is that when buying your clothes, for instance, you must avoid famous-name manufacturers and large chain retailers. This is not hard if you live in the kind of place that has plenty of vintage shops, such as your chosen Stoke Newington, Shoreditch or Notting Hill.

> **Sandra worked as a fairness liaison officer for Haringey Council, but in her spare time liked to tell people she disagreed with that she was going to kill them**

At this point it would be helpful to define some terms. By vintage I mean second-hand but more expensive than new. It really won't do to go to your nearest Sue Ryder shop, deck yourself in used clothes from M&S and then expect any credibility in an artisan coffee shop. The truth is that the gulf of difference between vintage and second-hand is as vast and unnavigable as the disparity between Jarvis Cocker and Jedward. But sadly, if you need me to explain that, then you may as well take off your ironic beanie and hand it round for the real hipsters to be sick in because you have already failed.

There are some quick and easy ways of identifying a vintage outfitters (as opposed to a straightforward second-hand shop) that can help you save time.

1. Unlike second-hand shops, vintage shops tend not to be named after a fatal disease. It is a small but important distinction that someone somewhere in the world of pre-loved couture came up with. Perhaps the idea came about as the result of a brainstorming session in which the new owner was suddenly inspired and said, 'I know, how about not calling it the Bowel Cancer Shop? Let's go for something a bit more fun, like, I dunno, the Retro Store? And then let's not donate the proceeds. Let's use the money to pay ourselves to run it instead of cynically relying on lonely old volunteers.' As a result, the vibe is very different because the staff are motivated by a living wage rather than having nothing better to do for two mornings a week.

2. Vintage shops specialise. So, in the window of the Retro Store will be a display of the coolest clothes ever. As if James Dean and Audrey Hepburn had dropped by, donated what they were wearing and casually arranged it around a 1950s Lambretta. Your average charity shop, on the other hand, has no option but to diversify, its stock being mostly derived from probate clearances. Hence, in their window you will likely see a headless mannequin dressed like a social worker, next to a display of I ♥ Blood Donors tea towels, a guitar, two squash rackets, some *Midsomer Murders* videos and a slightly grimy Kenwood mixer.

3. Vintage shops give you really nice brown-paper logoed carrier bags that you can walk down the street with, proud to know that everyone who sees it will know that you are an individual of style and taste, regardless of what you actually bought.

Charity shops generally send you packing with your nasty purchase in a plastic bag. Not a good one that might survive more than one sortie, but one of those cheap and flimsy ones that end up in dolphins' stomachs.

So, I should now turn my attention to the problem that you came to me with. Byron, you have grown a beard, only to find that it is a different colour from the hair on your head. I am sorry to hear this as I can only imagine how awkward it is to be looked at in the street by people who don't mean to be rude, but nevertheless cause considerable stress. Kids can be even worse, I bet? Too young to know better, but old enough to point and shout stuff like, 'Look at that funny man with the joke-shop beard and trousers that don't cover his ankles . . . He's not a real clown. Why is he in fancy dress, Mummy?' So cruel.

Make no mistake, this is somewhat of an emergency because your entire identity and rationale are at stake here. If you shave off the beard you will surely lose credibility in your community, but if you don't deal with the colour disparity, that same community will start to reject you, the way weak members of a lion pack get ostracised. I've seen it all too often on David Attenborough and it's heartbreaking – certainly not what we want to see happening to you. I actually do a very good Attenborough impression, but for the purposes of these pages, you will have to take my word for that. Were I able to demonstrate, I think it would go something like this:

(*In Attenborough voice*) The zebra succumbs to the chase and the lions can eat. Jack, the king of the pride, has first dibs; then his lioness and the rest of the family. But not Byron. He is no longer welcome due to his mane being the wrong colour and not matching the rest of his coat. He will have to find his own dinner. What an idiot . . . (*credits roll, sad music etc.*)

Dye is your next option but you will have to decide whether to go full ginger or full brown. It's really a matter of personal preference but I am imagining that having identified as brown-haired all your life until this red imposter took over your face, you will be wanting to correct that rather than your head hair. The jeopardy here is getting the colours to match sufficiently well so that the process does not exacerbate the problem. Get it wrong and you will be no happier with your new synthetic look than you are with the natural freak status you currently have to live with.

Of course, you have a third choice and it is one that you should give some weighty thought to as it is a brave one. Many readers will be thinking that a red beard would be something to be very pleased with, and I find myself agreeing. The trouble is that in your case, the look is cancelled by a mop of drab brownness like a cowpat that's landed on a bowl of strawberries (which can happen if you choose the wrong spot for your picnic, trust me). So your third choice is to shave your head. The 'bald but bearded' look is revered in many fashionable circles, all of which intersect to create a Venn sweet spot of pure, flawless hipsterism reserved for only the most perfect specimens. In this state, you will have achieved north-east London's idea of nirvana. It will inspire many to follow your example. You will be the human equivalent of Fairtrade coffee. Walk tall, Byron. With one simple trip to the barber you can be admired throughout Stoke Newington.

> Hi Jack, My flatmate and I take it in turn to cook and whoever doesn't cook does the dishes. The problem is that I am a very tidy cook and leave hardly any clearing-up for him to do whereas he leaves the kitchen looking like a bomb site. He just doesn't see that this is unfair. How do I persuade him?
>
> (Via SMS)

He doesn't see because you haven't shown him. Next time you cook, help him to understand by trashing the kitchen. Fill the blender with ketchup, leave the lid off and turn it on with a broom handle, use every dish you own and spill flour all over the tomatoey work surfaces, block the sink, sabotage the hot water and fill the Fairy Liquid bottle with Golden Syrup. When he's having his breakdown, gently suggest that you do the dishes together from now on. That way you can gradually teach him how to use the kitchen like a normal house-trained grown-up.

> *Hi Jack, I feel that I am on a slippery slope as three years ago I started shoplifting. It started with groceries but I soon graduated to clothes and became skilled at removing security tags. I have now got to the point where I am stealing electronic goods of high value and making a living by selling them on the internet. I never intended things to go this far and I really want it to stop before I get into serious trouble. Can you help?*
>
> *(Via SMS)*

Shoplifting is a recognised addiction and there are plenty of resources out there to address this, such as twelve-step programmes. I suggest you research it online and find a group near you that you like the look of. There is also specialised private therapy available; however, this can be costly. If it helps at all, I'll pay a fair price for an iPad Pro 12.9-inch, preferably black, but not a deal-breaker. Text me to arrange details.

Hi Jack. My wife Meg and I have been presented with a dilemma that we are hoping you can help us with. We have a five-year-old dog called Mini who is the apple of our eye. She is a rescue and of no obvious breed but very affectionate and well behaved (generally!). Mini gets plenty of exercise as we get up early to walk her. Also, I work from home, so she has company all day and is very contented. So, we have a neighbour who has proposed a dog-walking scheme whereby on Mondays and Wednesdays we walk her incredibly excitable and unpredictable terrier, Spike, with Mini, and on Tuesdays and Fridays she walks Mini with Spike. (Her boyfriend looks after Spike on Thursdays.) There are many reasons that we don't want to do this but we don't know how to tell our neighbour without coming across as unhelpful or standoffish as it was thoughtful of her to ask us. How do we get out of the arrangement without causing offence? Thanks in advance,

Holly and Meg (and Mini x)

Well, Holly, in many ways this is a classic dilemma. I have helped many people in the past who have found themselves in a similar situation, typically with a school run, but the dog-walking question is an increasingly common one, and one which throws up all the same issues. Hardly surprising because, as everyone knows, dogs are like children but way more rewarding and appreciative.

> **For a clever dog, having to walk with someone like Spike would be like serving a community payback sentence**

You don't list your reasons for not wanting in on this scheme, but I'm confident that I know them already so perhaps a good starting point would be to look at these as it will help you to see things in a clearer way, which, in turn will inform your choice of words when you respond to your neighbour's request.

You and Meg enjoy looking after Mini; it means that you walk together every morning and Mini is a very happy dog because she has a routine. It is to your credit that you have incorporated Mini's needs into a healthy lifestyle that benefits all three of you. For whatever reason, your neighbour has failed to do this and therefore sees her dog's needs from a different perspective: as a chore to be accomplished and preferably outsourced. If you go along with her proposal you lose in several ways: you compromise your enjoyable daily walks and you submit yourself to a needless commitment and the hassle that goes with it. Furthermore, twice a week, your dog gets walked by someone who obviously thinks walking a dog is a pain in the arse.

After all the wonderful things that you have done for Mini – rescuing her from a life surrounded by the bars of a pen and providing her with love and security – it could be disastrous now to abuse her trust by handing her over to your neighbour. Mini loves you and Meg; she doesn't give a used doggy bag for this neighbour or for the manic, inbred Spike. For a clever dog, having to walk with someone like Spike would be like serving a community payback sentence – she'll wonder what she did wrong and how long she will have to be lumped with this terrible neighbour for punishment. Because dogs can't actually say words, they were given eyes that speak instead, and Mini's eyes will be saying: 'Why? I thought you liked going on walks with me. Guess I was wrong about that, like I was wrong about my last owner who abandoned me in a lay-by. Is that what you're going to do to me next? Maybe I was wrong to ever think you were the answer to my prayers. Just one thing, when you do dump me on the roadside somewhere, please can I keep the collar you gave me, to remind me of the happiest days of my life? I'm sorry if I did anything wrong. And, in case I don't get a chance to say this, I'll always love you, Holly and Meg. Even if you decided you ultimately didn't love me after all. Goodbye.'

OK, that's a lot for even a dog's eyes to say in one fleeting glance but we all know how expressive they can be and how guilty they are capable of making us feel. Hopefully, by now you will have stopped reading, your eyes brimming with tears, and gone to find Mini, to lie down with her in her basket and whisper in her floppy, soft ears, 'I'm never ever going to hand you to anybody else for walkies,' before smothering her with contrite kisses.

When you come back to the end of my reply, your face still wet with tears of remorse and Mini's absolving licks, consider also the issue of intrusion that accompanies any such arrangement with a neighbour or even friend. My advice is not to let people like this into your world. Once you've opted in on something like dog walking, it will only be a matter of time before she tries it on further. 'Seeing as you've got the mower out anyway, I don't suppose you could just give my lawn the once-over, could you?' Or, 'Big favour, I know, but can I pop this turkey in your freezer until Xmas, only mine's full?' Or, 'Bit of a cheeky one, but I couldn't just charge my Tesla on your mains, could I? I'd use my own only for some reason my bill's sky-high already.' I am only saying that this could happen. There's no need to panic if it does, mind. People who are brazen enough to endlessly cadge and beg favours are absolutely always too thick-skinned to be upset by a refusal. They live by the blaggers' mantra: 'Don't ask: don't get', and it's important that they learn pretty quickly that *your* mantra is very much: 'Don't ask.'

Your neighbour is likely to be one of those unoffendable thick-skins who will shake off rejection like Mini shakes off rain. Good timing is useful in these instances. An ideal example of the succinct conversation you should have with her goes as follows:

NEIGHBOUR

Oh hello, Holly, just the person. I don't suppose
I could ask you to—

YOU

(*loudly with hand raised as if stopping traffic*):

No.

(*And walk away.*)

NEIGHBOUR

(*cheerily, undaunted*)

No worries at all. Just thought I'd ask. See you
soon, Byeeee.

Meg, you had the wisdom and faith to entrust me with your predicament and to help you find a way out of it, so I really hope you follow this advice in a similar spirit. I am totally on your side. You have created a family unit that is perfect for all three of you. Nobody, least of all a chaotic, clingy neighbour can be allowed to dismantle that. By all means help out and walk her dog on the odd occasion because that is the proper role of a neighbour, but resist at all costs being sucked into the unimagineable vortex of incompetence that is her day-to-day life. And by 'odd occasion' I mean if she has to, say, visit her sick mother because she's taken a turn for the worse. Even then, ask for proof – like a note from the nursing home. Or make it plain that, upon her return, you expect to be provided with a photo of her with her bedridden mother holding that day's newspaper. It's only fair that you have confirmation that you are not spending the morning trying to pull rabid Spike off passing joggers and cyclists while she is at a spa gulping Prosecco and laughing with her chums. Be bold, Holly, because this is nothing short of a war in which there can only be one victor. Make sure it's you.

We don't have enough sex since our children were born as they are always waking up and calling out or just running into our room at the wrong time. It's awkward and quite a turn-off. What do you suggest?

(Via SMS)

This is a common problem with a simple solution: turn the radio up and lock your bedroom door. Or theirs. If they persist, I suggest randomly running into their room and wrecking something that *they're* enjoying, like a Lego project. Hopefully they'll get the message eventually. If not, get a babysitter and book yourselves into a hotel. Depending how romantic or perfunctory you want to be, you can go from a suite at the Savoy to an Ibis on an hourly rate.

I know this sounds stupid but since binge-watching Homeland I have developed this phobia that my house has been bugged and that I am constantly under surveillance. What should I do about it?

Please be assured that this is almost certainly an unwarranted fear, but just to be on the safe side, keep your curtains drawn, don't use the phone and play loud music if you want to have a private conversation in your house. Above all, trust no one.

Dear Jack. At 52, I worry that even if things ever do return to normal after Covid, I never will. Before the lockdown my husband and I used to eat out once a month with friends who are all saying that they are looking forward to doing that again but the sight of waiters in masks and so on has put me off forever. I don't want to be a killjoy and realise that I am luckier than many and some friends say I should count my blessings but I can't get enthusiastic. Please can you advise me?

Lynn, Stafford

It has all been a bit of a turn-off, hasn't it, Lynn? I don't really fancy eating out either. This reluctance was not helped by reading about someone who discovered that one of her takeaway chicken nuggets was in fact a face mask scrunched up inside a ball of batter. A kind of dystopian Kinder Egg for our time.

The restaurant business, quite possibly more than any other, is ill equipped to deal with this crisis because eating out is so closely related to the ideas of togetherness, relaxing and the joy of living. For example, one of my favourite puddings, cheesecake, is a wicked treat, the more so because of the flagrant disregard for our health it embodies. The act of consuming it is a celebration of the present and a deliberate defiance of all the consequences. But that act of rebellion is deep-cleaned away by the vision of waiters dressed in scrubs, sliding the plate across the table towards us as if it's hospital waste. I'd lay a bet that nobody has proposed marriage in a restaurant since coronavirus crawled onto the scene. There can be no romance within a hundred metres of a hand sanitiser and industrial tripod-mounted thermometer. There is no whimsical fun in ordering champagne from someone wearing a hazmat visor.

Of course, you are quite right that you are luckier than many but that doesn't disqualify you from the benefit of my professional opinion. And being told to count your blessings can often seem like a dismissal of your concerns rather than a thoughtful reflection upon them.

In fact, a word about those people in our lives who speak in aphorisms, glibly spouting off proverbial wisdoms as a balm to any problem. This is cheap, lazy and singularly unhelpful for someone seeking real answers. It's flat-pack advice that should come with the warning 'self-assembly required'. It is advice that says: 'I'm not clever enough to help you specifically but I do have a handful of generic quotes that sometimes enable me to give the impression that I can empathise with other people and even have something useful to contribute.' A wise listener should be able to tailor a response to your specific needs and not just quote fridge magnets at you. Next time you need proper, considered advice from someone and they fob you off with a saying like, 'The longest journey begins with a single step,' throw it back at them. Just say, 'Thanks for that. Next time I won't waste my time explaining my problems to you, I'll just go and browse round a branch of Clintons until I see the right little ditty.'

Anyway, back to your problem, Lynn. Perhaps none of us can expect to return to the past and pick up from where we left off as if nothing happened. We should undoubtedly brace ourselves for a future that will be shaped by the events of 2020. We cannot unknow what we have learnt from this experience. Washing our hands is here to stay. So boring, but there you have it. And 'boring' is the operative word. In the aftermath of 9/11 we all saw that the world was going to be different, and so it is, but really only in all the tedious aspects of air travel that now blight every plane journey. Because of that terrible day we now have to take our shoes and belts off and shuffle through airport security holding our trousers up while trying to maintain the dignified cool of an international traveller. A similarly diminishing effect will be brought about by the pandemic. The regulations imposed upon us so quickly will not be taken away without leaving a permanent stain on our lives. Businesses and individuals will stockpile hand sanitiser and PPE, fearful of future shortages. Cupboards will bulge with emergency toilet rolls, giving the impression of a nation of bum-obsessed preppers. People will be reluctant to have physical contact, to shake hands or hug. Even now there's a vaccine and the risk is dramatically lowered, why take the chance of getting other infections when health is now seen as so fragile?

On the plus side, all this new contact avoidance brings with it the small advantage of not having to negotiate our way through the unclear greeting etiquette that changes with the seasons. Should we shake hands, do elbows, hug or kiss? Should it be a double kiss and, if so, left cheek then right or vice versa? In

Britain it seems to be the one custom that we dispensed with quite readily. We were understandably outraged by 10 p.m. last orders and clothes being deemed non-essential shopping by HM Government but there seemed to be a collective sense of relief at the prohibition of touch. Our reversion to the uncomplicated nod has come as a welcome replacement for the twee face-dance that is air-kissing. And, please God, save us from the desperate pretension of that multiphased handshake that is occasionally imposed on one. Probably it's a bloke thing, but you know what I'm talking about, Lynn.

It's that completely unnecessary ritual of endless different thumb grips and knuckle clenches that takes an unfeasibly long time and achieves nothing but a sense of failure when clumsily executed by the uninitiated. Admittedly, it looks quite cool if you're in an episode of *The Wire*, but not if you're actually at a barbecue in

> **Our reversion to the uncomplicated nod has come as a welcome replacement for the twee face-dance that is air-kissing**

Surrey. Frankly, if you're over twenty-five, white and middle class and you want to do a fancy handshake with your mates, just join the Masons and stop pretending to be down with the brothers. In all other areas, I think that the argument condemning cultural appropriation is a segregationist's wet dream but in this specific instance I'd say its champions do have a point.

So I hope that you will see from what I have said in a roundabout way so far that your anxieties are merely sensible predictions. Looked at another way, it would be odd to believe that you would be able to carry on as if nothing happened. To use another tortuous analogy, if you'd been involved in a train crash it's only reasonable to expect that future travel by rail would not be the relaxed, carefree experience it once was. Every sudden jolt or strange noise would bring with it a sense of threat that it previously would not have done. Of course, one obvious way to neutralise that fear would be only to travel with Network SouthEast as their trains are too slow ever to cause concern. But, more practically, I would ask you to consider the following: you can't stop your world from changing but you can control the way that you respond to that change. (And I didn't get that from a fridge magnet. It was on a quite tasteful poster with a picture of a sunset that was a gift from a grateful client. Well, I say 'gift' it was among his possessions when he was led away having been convicted of aggravated assault on a Clintons security guard. His lawyer took the magnets.)

Give yourself some time to adjust to the new world that we are emerging into. Get acquainted with the unfamiliar ways that it heralds. Do not expect so much of yourself too soon and observe that nobody is inclined to mark getting the jab with a slap-up dinner in a smart restaurant. Humankind has had the rug pulled from beneath its feet so you are not alone in not trusting the red-carpet treatment just yet. Best wishes to you, Lynn.

I have discovered my wife is having an affair when I noticed she was receiving a lot of texts from someone at work. I haven't told her I know yet because I am still getting my head around it. I'm scared she'll leave me, but at the same time I'm not sure I'll ever get over the lies. How can I confront her? And how can I ever learn to trust her again if she tells me the affair is over?

(Via SMS)

To recap: she's getting texts from work so that means she's having an affair, she's going to leave you and you'll never get over her lies. At least get some facts before engaging in this imagination triple jump. Unless you've noticed that your wife tends to reply to these texts with a topless selfie I'd say you are worrying unnecessarily. Most work-related texts are unbelievably dull and are about things like sales targets and whose turn it is to tidy the stationery cupboard. In fact if she is sending pornographic images in reply to messages like that, then you should be pleased that you are married to someone with a sense of humour.

Greetings, Jack. For some time now I have been considering contacting the agony aunt in our daily paper about this problem, but then Jean, my wife, spotted an item about how you were compiling this so we thought we would give you a go, so to speak. What it is, is that for three years now, Jean and I have included our neighbour Barry on lots of social events, outings and trips etc. He is about our age and we are all retired so have plenty of time for recreation of this sort. The trouble is that we always end up paying for everything. It's not just the teas and coffees but also things like entrance fees if we go on a garden tour sometimes. Also, I always drive and so there is the fuel and parking costs to think of. It can really add up and Jean and I are getting fed up with it yet don't know how to bring up the matter and get Barry to pay his share. He is a widower and that is why we have taken him under our wing, so to speak, and don't want to upset him but also feel enough is enough. Can you suggest how we get around this? Many thanks.

Graham, Mill Hill

Well, 'greetings', Graham, as you evidently say in Mill Hill. Thank you for your letter. I can assure you that this is not an unusual problem. From the mate who doesn't buy his round to the colleague at work who, seeing that you are nipping out to Fynn's coffee shop, casually asks, 'Couldn't grab me a latte, could you? Caramel topper. Thanks, bud.' No mention of remuneration but you get him his drink anyway. Heck, what's £2.30 anyway? (Answer: it's £2.30. The same as it was last week, and the week before. So I suppose it's £6.90 so far. Not that it matters, you think to yourself.)

Only, the next day he sneaks out and returns with his solo cuppa and a Danish and sits at his desk dunking and sipping away, really enjoying it, without a care in the world. And you find yourself daydreaming that you have just seen a news alert that Fynn's have issued an urgent recall notice owing to choke hazards being found in their pastries. It's a long story but somehow a box of trachea-sized plastic discs accidentally got spilt into the mix along with the raisins and nuts. Exhilarated, you say nothing and quietly wait a while until you hear the soft *plip* of a cardboard cup dropping to the ground and spilling its contents. Then the powerless rasp of desperately needed breath, the crash of a swivel chair upturned by a falling body and a pudgy hand losing its grip on the edge of the desk, leaving a smudge of blueberry icing. You give it a good two minutes and then, 'Everything OK, mate?' you ask, leaning round the partitioning screen, knowing that there will be no reply.

Now, obviously, all of that is a fictional account of the kind of ill will that is generated by someone who won't pay their way or reciprocate the generosity of those around them. As you have already discovered for yourself, Barry's meanness causes extraordinary levels of resentment that can consume your every waking hour. Therefore it is really important that we look at why you got into this strange relationship in the first place so that you can find a way of resolving the problem.

At first, retirement for some people seems like a holiday, even a second honeymoon, but after a while the sense of freedom gives way to an unending series of trials. In fact the metaphor I would use for retirement is that of being on one of those luxury cruises that are always being advertised on ITV.

Everything starts very well: there are loads of activities, a choice of restaurants, two cinemas, a health centre and even a theatre that does cabaret and musicals, which will hopefully give you plenty of opportunities to get to know some of the other passengers. The first week flies by and you can hardly believe how nice everything is. By the middle of week two you're still enjoying yourselves but you decide to cut down on the food just a little bit and try to take more exercise. The gym is much busier than in the brochure so you take up walking on deck instead. On the third day of doing this, you change your route just to vary the routine a bit and maybe meet some different people.

The weather is nice and sometimes there is an announcement to explain that a small island that neither of you has heard of can be seen from A Deck or that someone's inhaler has been found by the Poseidon Bar on C Deck and can be claimed at lost property on G Deck. It's all very friendly and well organised. The only slight drawback is that your daily sorties have begun to impress upon you both that, although the liner is very big – the second biggest in the fleet, apparently – it is, nevertheless, a ship surrounded by sea. 'Trapped' is a strong word, but for some reason you find yourself muttering it, quite involuntarily, from time to time.

The reason I have described retirement in these terms, Graham, is that so many people can't see why it makes them dissatisfied and, in turn, this causes them to look for fresh stimuli that will address their underlying sadness. Might it be that you and Jean are a bit like the couple on that cruise, always seeking new activities and people to chat with? To be blunt, it could be that one or both of you reached out to Barry through boredom and a hope that his company would brighten things up for you.

If that is the case, then it is one of those conundrums that solves itself. You can simply stop including old moth-pockets Barry and get on with finding some better friends. And you don't have to do this unkindly. I'm not suggesting for a moment that you go round, ring the bell and when he comes to the door say, 'Oh, hi, Barry. Just to say, me and Jean won't be doing anything else with you from now on. If saving a few bob here and a couple of quid there is so important to you then why don't you take your precious pension and shove it up your jacksie?' That would be unspeakably vulgar and wrong. It should, of course, be 'Jean and I'.

However, it would be unprofessional of me not to consider the other likely reason that you and your wife have shared so much of your time with your neighbour. Namely, that you have taken Barry under your wing out of a sense of pity. On one level this is to your credit. Unfortunately, your kindness has backfired because, for his own reasons, Barry sees it the other way round. He is convinced that he is doing you and Jean a favour by gracing *you* with *his* company and that it seems only fair that you cover his expenses. This is a knottier problem to resolve as it will require a delicate handling of the facts if you wish to salvage the friendship.

One way to begin the process of resetting things on more equitable terms is to work out all the costs of your next shared trip in advance, not forgetting to include the little hidden expenses such as boiled sweets. Don't worry about causing offence because I suspect you will find that Barry is pretty thick-skinned and sees the odd veiled insult as the occupational hazard of a seasoned cheat (and, let's face it, that is what he is). He'll just roll with the punches, you watch. Explain you'll need £15 for petrol, up front, like now, adding something along the lines of, 'Tell you what, why don't you have a few minutes with your cash so you can say your goodbyes?' He might not actually find it amusing but I guarantee he'll pretend to as he realises that you're on to him.

It could just be that this is enough to bring Barry to his senses, see how petty and ungenerous he has been towards his kindly neighbours and mend his ways. I must say that I am not persuaded that this will happen, judging from what you have told me about his personality. Old dog, new tricks and all that. A more likely outcome is that he will abandon your company and move on to find a different couple to sponge from. All the best, Graham. And thanks for writing.

Hi Jack. Although my mates tell me I am shy, I don't feel that I truly am, but at the same time feel I don't really fit in with them. I do sort of like my mates and have known them since school but I have begun to find them brash and loud. They often chant songs when they come out of the pub late at night and even start fights sometimes. When I try to calm them down, they accuse me of being a chicken or gay. Another thing is that none of them talk about anything other than sport, sex and what is on television. At 28, I find behaviour like that a bit boring and I suppose I always did. What should I do to feel like I fit in more?

Ryan, St Albans

Ryan, hello. I don't think I will be alone in reading your letter and immediately wanting to say, 'You shouldn't try to fit in. Your friends are dicks. Move on.' However, that would be a case of easier said than done, I suspect. You have known these people all your life. You live and socialise in a fairly small town so it is going to be hard for you to extract yourself from their company and start again with a new set of people. Hard, but not impossible, and so that is one area that we will look at. I should make it clear from the start that I am not in any way singling out St Albans as problematic. I would give the same advice to somebody from Aylesbury as well. And Letchworth.

It is actually a rare thing for anybody to develop a close friendship in early life that continues to grow throughout adulthood. The usual pattern is that we mature in different ways and adapt our network accordingly. Your particular case differs slightly in that you have matured and they haven't. I won't go into the neuroscience behind this, even though I could if I wanted to, as it won't help you with your dilemma. But I can summarise it for our purposes here. The major landmark in human maturation, it will not surprise you to learn, is adolescence. This normally commences in males at about the age of eleven and will continue for around eight to ten years. However, this can go on much longer, as appears to be the case with your friends. The reasons for this can be genetic (you have an inherited condition that delays/prevents maturation); experiential (you are emotionally damaged by an event or factors in your past such as being unpopular at school); environmental (your surroundings and company are not conducive to mental development); or a combination of all three, in which case you're probably a presenter on Radio 1.

So, usually, by around the age of twenty-one the male adult character has emerged and is able to distinguish between childish and mature behaviour. None of which happened in the case of your friends, which is why they appear to be trapped in a twilight world of banter, lager, punch-ups and unfeasibly tight jeans.

You need to explore new friendships and settings in order to achieve a sense of belonging and contentment. I would urge you to consider this a priority and not just something that can be addressed as and when the opportunity arises. Unfortunately, the clarity with which you currently see your situation cannot be relied upon as a source of momentum for change. Before long, if no progress is made, your subconscious will stop appealing for better company and proper conversation. Instead it will give up, having concluded that this must be all that life has to offer and maybe even all that you are capable of – an endless cycle of pub crawls and joshing; loud, empty beer-chat about errant referees, big knockers and so-and-so's new car. You will start joining in as your inner soul shrinks away, concluding that you might as well because there is nothing else. And so you become one of those who, knowing he has nothing to say, starts shouting instead.

Which brings us back to your question of what you should do to fit in. In a sense, the answer is, literally, nothing. Stop seeing these 'mates' and find a new world to inhabit. By all means be sensitive to their feelings as you go about it. But don't agonise over it. Their emotional range doesn't encompass the capacity to feel hurt by your withdrawal. Any slight grievance will quickly wash out with the second pint and you will be forgotten.

Your next task is to find some way of building a new life that will allow you to branch out, to think and to develop as a person. If that all sounds a bit too Californian, please don't worry, I am not trying to trick you into taking up reiki therapy, male bonding and drinking your own urine, all of which are pointless and weird and I suspect started off as practical jokes. No, my suggestion is to take up a hobby to expand your social circle and, by so doing, drift away from your current acquaintances. But go slowly to begin with. It will help you reorientate and give you time to filter out the duds that you will inevitably meet along the way. Good luck, Ryan. Also, leave St Albans.

> Some time ago my then girlfriend dumped me quite suddenly and I later found out that she had moved in with someone who was much better looking and more successful than me. It hasn't done much for my confidence and I want to know how to get some self-esteem back.
>
> (Via SMS)

I bet you do.

Jack, does life begin at 40? I am approaching it fast.

(Via SMS)

Whoever tells you life begins at forty very obviously wasted the first forty years of their life. As Pink Floyd said on *Dark Side of the Moon*, 'No one told you when to run . . . you missed the starting gun'. (That was from one of her better albums, before she ditched the surname and just started calling herself 'Pink', dyed her hair and tried to appeal to a younger market. Big mistake. She was probably having a mid-life crisis like you are.)

Hi Jack, I am a single mum and live in a terraced house with my two teenage sons. The problem is that my neighbours are constantly complaining to me about them. Sometimes they will come to the door and have a moan and other times, for instance when the music is too loud, they will bang on the wall quite aggressively. I honestly think that my boys are well behaved and I don't just ignore it if they do get noisy as I have a go at them and they quieten down. Our other neighbours agree that the boys are pretty good and we don't have trouble with anyone else in the street. I don't want to fall out with our neighbours but don't know how to deal with them when they start going on at me. As they are over 70, during the first lockdown, my boys even went up to the chemists for them quite a few times but it hasn't made any difference and now they are back to complaining. What should I do?

Kylie, Hull

Thank you for writing to me, Kylie. I have forwarded your name and address to Hull social services who have been in touch to confirm that the best thing is for your sons to be taken into juvenile custody for public order offences and are now processing your case.

Just kidding. Seriously, the way I see it is that you have two normal teenage boys. Unfortunately, you also have two normal elderly neighbours and my task is to help you to find a way of dealing with the friction that is caused when they clash. For the sake of my reply, I will refer to the neighbours as Mr and Mrs Gripe. Hardly inventive or amusing, I know – a bit twee, in fact – but my first choice has been vetoed by the publishers who say that I have already used up my quota of foul language for this book.

When I started reading your letter, I have to admit there was a part of me that was thinking I would have to suggest ways for you to rein in your boys. It sounded like a simple case of thoughtless teens versus harmless couple next door. We all know how out of control teenagers can become, especially when they're high as satellites on whatever is in those little SodaStream cartridges you see all over the ground in swing parks. I suppose I should count myself lucky that illegal drugs and substance abuse were a rarity when I was growing up. Doubly lucky, in fact, in that the owner of a certain convenience store my friends and I frequented had no compunction about selling us cigarettes and vodka. His age test was apparently whether or not you could see over the counter. So it was that we were able to puff and swig our way into a swirling frenzy of vomiting. You see, we made our own entertainment in those days . . .

As I was saying, I thought it was going to be a case of your boys against the Gripes and that I was merely needed to adjudicate. However, the more I read, the more I realised that you have every right to be upset by your neighbours' intolerance. The fact is that you have raised two fine young citizens who, naturally enough, get a bit rowdy at times, but who, responding to the call of a national crisis made it their business to look out for the two old prunes next door. It makes the blood boil to think of their kind actions being met with unrelenting negativity: 'Here's your prescription, Mr Gripe.' 'Yeah? Well you still can't have your ball back, now clear off before I call the police . . . Go on, f*** off.' Not exactly the stuff of John Lewis Christmas adverts, is it?

In fact, I have made a mental note to myself, Kylie, that as I approach my seventh decade (I know, physique and looks-wise I've been blessed) I will make doubly sure that I maintain my generous and happy-go-lucky outlook. One day in my old age, I might find myself living next door to youngsters like your own and I very much hope that they will know and think of me as 'That nice Mr Dee who has taught us so much with his kind nature and zest for life'.

Alas, it is too late for the Gripes. Their retirement is a dreary cycle of heating up soup, cleaning out the cat litter and watching repeats of *Bergerac* at a volume that would embarrass Cineworld. It's a drudgery relieved only by waiting for your children's next transgression so that they can trigger another volley of indignation in your direction. The more they go on, the more reassuring it is to hear the sound of their own voices asserting their existence, but for that they need an audience. Unfortunately, in this case that audience is you. I could suggest baking them a cake and taking it round; sometimes a spontaneous gesture like that can achieve wonderful results. However, I suspect from the way your sons' errand-running was received that your kindness would be rejected with similar obtuseness. There is no pleasing this couple. It'll no doubt be the wrong flavour or contain something they can't eat. You may as well bake the cake, cover it in whipped cream, pop round with it and when Mr Gripe opens the door, splat it in his miserable face. At least then they'd have something real to complain about.

They have painted you, quite wrongly, as the neighbour from

hell, giving you two options. You can deny it and try to prove otherwise. (Been there, done that, didn't work. Any normal person would be heartily grateful for two lads to run up to Superdrug and get their Preparation H for them. Not Mr and Mrs Gripe.) Or you can own it. Become the menace they believe you to be. In all likelihood they are already bad-mouthing you and the kids – there's nothing you can do about it, so why not at least have the satisfaction of saying you did those things of which you are accused?

Imagine what a tonic it will be for you when you walk to the shops and somebody says, 'Oh watcha, Kylie. Is it true you went round and twatted Mr Gripe with a cake?' To which you can hold your head high and say, 'Yep. That was me, he had it coming, the whingey old bastard.' One or two others will overhear and tell you they'd have done the same and that they've heard you play incredibly loud, aggressive music all night long. You'll say it's true, even though it's not, and you'll enjoy their look of admiration.

Obviously, don't take it too far or you and the boys could attract unwanted media attention with headlines like 'Neighbours from Hull' (*Daily Mail*) or 'Teens Terrorise Estate' (*Sun*) and 'Benefits Scum Family Need Locking Up' (*Guardian*). Yes, it surprised me as well, that last one. Following on will be the inevitable film crew making a fly-on-the-wall documentary series because some

> **'Imagine what a tonic it will be for you when you walk to the shops and somebody says, 'Oh watcha, Kylie. Is it true you went round and twatted Mr Gripe with a cake?'**

executive read about you and thought that everyone should see how gritty real life is in the north-east. Get the balance right between being considerate and showing a humorous disregard for your neighbours' more unreasonable complaints and I predict you could become a reality star, recognised as a new kind of folk hero battling to raise her sons against the odds. Good luck.

Dear Jack, I left my decent job because I was itching for a change and the chance to run my own business. Turns out it is pretty bloody hard and lonely out in the wild. I want to ask for my old job back but my pride is getting in the way. Any advice on how I can go back to how things were and still save face?

(Via SMS)

So far you haven't been too proud to admit failure, being work-shy or unpopular. I think you'll manage asking for your job back. For an alternative approach read my letter to Vihaan from Luton.

Dear Jack. For the last two years a colleague (who I will call Col) and I have taken it in turns to drive to work as we live only one road apart. It does have the advantage of reducing the cost of fuel etc. and although we are not friends as such we get on all right. The thing that ruins this arrangement is that Col is actually a shocking driver. He seems hardly aware of other road users, quite often texts as he is going along, and never goes slower than 60 on a 40mph stretch that we have to go along. Last week he took the wing mirror off a parked car as he turned a corner and all he did was say 'Ooops. Was that us?', didn't stop and never even mentioned it again. Every time he drives I find myself gripping the edge of my seat and occasionally screwing my eyes shut. It can be quite terrifying and I often get to work feeling shattered. He seems completely unaware of the stress he is causing me and other road users but I feel that I can't say anything to him as he is senior to me at work and a lot older and yet I can't think of a way of cancelling the arrangement without it coming across as a snub. Please can you help?

Neil, Coventry

Hello Neil. I sympathise. This is an awkward situation and one that needs to be resolved fairly urgently before a serious accident occurs. And I don't just mean one relating to your trousers. At the risk of being presumptuous, I would also suggest that the dilemma is deepened by your Englishness. It's hard to think of nationals from other countries who would prioritise not wishing to cause offence over their personal safety in a potentially life-threatening situation. Obviously I am very well travelled and have been blessed with great powers of observation as well as an uncanny ear for accents. This means I am able to give you a flavour of the range of reactions you might get from around the world without having to resort to crude stereotypes like most other writers would. In Australia, for example, it would be something like, 'Strewth, mate, slow down or you're gonna hit another roo and I'll spill me Foster's again.' In Italy: *'Mama mia, slowa downa di Alfa Romeo or we a gonna be spaghetti.'* An American passenger would undoubtedly be chewing a match and say something along the lines of, 'Hey buddy, there's only one widow-maker in this Dodge and it's the one tucked in my snakeskin belt, so why don't you take your cowboy boot off the gas and cool the heck down 'fore I have to put some lead in that there skull of yours.' Three fictional, yet accurate vignettes that share one important common denominator in that the speaker is unabashed at telling the driver what he would like him to do. In England, however, that would not be the case and so it is that you find yourself praying for deliverance with your maniacal colleague each morning.

---

* I do not include Essex, where the passenger's reaction would be more, 'Come on, geeza, can't this fing go any faster?' (*loud bang*). 'Don't worry abaaaatt that, you only clipped him. Oh, 'ello. Now you gone and got the rozzers up yer arris, put yer foot daaaan or we'll be doin' bird for this.'

I have outlined all of this simply to identify the problem that you are facing. Bad driving is inexcusable and is the kind of behaviour that belongs in that category of serious but often unpunished wrongdoing that includes skyping in public, BO, talking in the cinema and tearing articles out of magazines at the doctor's.

Many feel that people should have to resit their driving test when they reach a certain age, but this strikes me as discriminatory. Statistically, most old people are very careful drivers who are at much lower risk of having an accident than the rest of us. Admittedly this is achieved by never going faster than 20mph, which is fair enough unless you're stuck behind their Nissan Micra, in which case you find yourself daydreaming about ordering a drone strike on it. A fairer system of testing for older drivers would be simply to make sure they can still see above the steering wheel. Driving so that your head can't be seen as your car glides past is, at the very least, troubling and, at worst, likely to cause accidents by distracting other motorists.

> **Admittedly this is achieved by never going faster than 20mph, which is fair enough unless you're stuck behind their Nissan Micra, in which case you find yourself daydreaming about ordering a drone strike on it**

Having said that, there is the other category of reckless driver who, for reasons I won't go into here, become more and more dangerous the longer they have been driving (it's basically everything from prescribed drug abuse to a costly divorce – like I say, let's not go there). My thinking is that Col belongs in this group. In all likelihood his dangerous driving will not be halted by anything other than a tree or a lamp post. The challenge for you is how not to be in the car when that happens.

Admittedly, this is a tricky one. Every solution is tangled in problems of its own. You can't confront Col because he almost certainly won't take it well from a junior, creating a bad vibe at work for you and initiating a campaign of subtle retribution, having used his status to commandeer the help of your department. Before very long he will have spread his propaganda, establishing you as a crybaby and scaredy-cat. It will probably only be a matter of days before you come back from lunch to discover a packet of XL Pampers has been placed on your desk and your screensaver has been changed to a gif of the Teletubbies waving from their stupid bubble car. This is the worst kind of bullying because it is designed to embarrass and to be more awkward to report than just quietly tolerate.

Nor can you just hand in your notice. It could damage your career, mark you permanently as a quitter, an unlikeable loner, volatile, prone to panic attacks and generally bone idle with a plank-sized chip on your shoulder. That's exactly the type who eventually ends up drifting into stand-up comedy. Believe me, Neil, it's not worth it.

Cycling might appear to be an obvious fix. You could announce that you are on a new fitness regime and, as much as you've enjoyed the lift sharing, the time has come for you to knuckle down and get your bike clips on. In all probability,

Col will be gracious, wish you luck and your dilemma will be solved. Dream on. There are so many reasons why this is a terrible solution. Firstly, Col is clearly a vindictive piece of work who is not psychologically equipped to handle rejection of this sort without planning his own form of vengeance that could well involve tampered brakes or a carefully positioned spill of grease on that sharp bend at the bottom of the (literally) last hill. Secondly, even if he doesn't actively seek retribution, remember you will now be riding a bicycle twice a day on the same road and at the same time as Col who, we already know, has little regard for human life, especially yours, and drives his car like he's just stolen it. Your long-term chances of surviving are slim to zero and you are far too young to join that great peloton in the sky. Thirdly, as the great Lance Armstrong will tell you, cycling is incredibly tough and impossible to do well without skip-loads of steroids. And fourthly, it denies you your right to that most basic human desire to arrive at work looking normal and not like a failed Marvel character. So, cycling is not the answer.

You could take an inventive approach and declare that you have decided to learn a second language, say, Spanish, via an app on your phone during your commute. Therefore, because you don't wish to cause annoyance, you propose ending the friendly arrangement (that you so enjoyed) of sharing the driving. That way, you will explain, you can practise your '¿Como estás?' and '¿Dónde está el baño?' in your car while he can listen to the radio in his. Notwithstanding Col's well-known violent mood swings and difficulty in accepting change, this solution is fraught with hazard. Don't forget that you will have to support your story with a demonstrable improvement in Spanish. Even worse, however, would be for Col to tell you that he'd love to learn as well and, 'Why don't we do it together?' Your problem will have doubled as he swerves traffic and pedestrians while shouting inane Spanish phrases. Apart from authentically replicating a cab ride through Madrid, you will have achieved nothing.

There is perhaps one recourse that, although radical, warrants consideration. In a nutshell, you should focus all your efforts on becoming a terrible driver. Find ways of making his journeys with you so frightening and stressful that the onus is on Col to bring the agreement to a close. Enlist a friend to drive too slowly in front so that you can toot him constantly until he gets out at a red light and threatens to kill you both with an axe if he ever sees your car again. As he returns to his vehicle you can worsen the showdown by shouting back at him, something like, 'Yeah? Well you're not the only one with an axe. Col here's got a samurai sword at home, so bring it on, you fat wanker. We'll be ready for you.' Then drive off, giving him the finger and telling Col how you can't wait to have a full-on knife fight with that idiot and that you will make sure the two of you are properly tooled up for the next time you see him. If Col starts spluttering at this point and is generally lost for words, mumbling things about having kids and so on, you will know that the ploy has worked and that it will only be a matter of days before he comes to you to regretfully say he has had to make other travel arrangements, or has taken up cycling/decided to learn Spanish and that it's been a pleasure etc. etc. You will have solved the problem and, who knows, if Col spreads the word, possibly have gained yourself a little bit of respect as being a hard nut that nobody wants to get on the wrong side of. The world could be your oyster. Bon voyage, Neil.

Dear Jack. When you hang your washing out, how do you arrange it on the line? Small to large, or by colour?

(Via SMS)

Sorry, I don't think we've met. My name is Jack and I have a life.

Hi Jack, I have found out by accident that my husband Mark is planning a surprise birthday party for me next year when I reach 50. I discovered this by taking a phone call from an indiscreet caterer who asked to speak with Mark, who was out, and when I offered to take a message he told me all the plans as he obviously did not know that it was meant to be a secret. Anyway, when it dawned on me that this is what Mark was organising, my blood practically ran cold. I can't think of anything worse than one of those big 'Surprise' moments you see in films and I am already dreading it to the extent that I am looking up how to fake being ill so I can get out of it. Please have you got any advice?

Kelly, Hull

Hello Kelly. I feel for you but I have to confess that my first thought was for Mark and the extraordinary bad luck he had in happening to find the Kim Philby of catering. It is a very well established and known fact that medicine, law, the priesthood, journalism and hospitality are the five vocations whose primary ethical principle is that of utmost integrity and discretion. Obviously doctors and nurses all have a bloody good laugh at our expense in their free time but generally they seem able to keep patients' names out of the frame.* Lawyers will scrupulously guard your confidences until they hit the wine bar of a Friday and then all bets are off. Fair enough. Priests can always be relied on to keep your secrets 100 per cent safe because they've had so much practice with their own. And journalists famously never disclose their sources – a noble pledge usually invoked to spare them the inconvenience of admitting they made it all up. But caterers? Surely it should go without saying that a discussion with a caterer would be subject to the highest standards of privacy. Speaking from my personal experience of working as a waiter in the 1980s when I had the honour of regularly serving and chatting with Princess Diana, I know that I would simply never disclose the details of those long, candid and very personal conversations we had about all the other members of the royal family. No sir. Not then. Not now. Not until I get the right book deal.

Hoteliers and restaurateurs have a strict code of conduct when it comes to sharing information and, besides, discretion is a quality that comes naturally to someone with a properly functioning common sense. What hotel employee in their right mind would call a landline number to confirm a booking and when

---

* Although it remains a mystery how a journalist contacted me, out of the blue, to ask about my health the very day after I had been prescribed medication to relieve the symptoms of a rectal fissure. The fact that the hack was clearly having trouble containing her hysterics *and* shared the same surname as my GP cannot be a coincidence, surely. I even considered complaining to the BMA to let it be known that a line has been crossed and I wasn't just going to sit there and take it. The truth is I wasn't actually able to sit anywhere at the time and once the discomfort had responded to the treatment, I was so grateful that I decided to let the matter drop.

asked if they would like to leave a message would say, 'Oh, just to say that Mr Robson's usual suite has been reserved with a bottle of his favourite champagne and extra body lotion as requested'? OK, full disclosure, I did it once when I was working at the Lexington in Mayfair but my reasoning was that Mr Robson never tipped and on one occasion clicked his fingers to get my attention. Well, he got it. And subsequently, a sudden and very expensive divorce. Nobody calls me 'sonny'.

I am not for one minute suggesting that a hasty divorce would solve your problem. Even though it clearly would. No, my working assumption is that, despite Mark's failed attempt at organising a party behind your back, you feel that he deserves another chance to prove he is still the man you married and that he hasn't, over the years, become a thoughtless idiot.

A word now about the nature of surprises as it might shed light on your dislike of them. Life holds enough surprises without our spouses creating bespoke ones for us. In fact, the only genuine surprise is that, occasionally, you get a nice one. Bumping into someone you haven't seen in years can be called a nice surprise. At least it can for the three or four minutes of catch-up chat it takes for you to recall *why* you haven't seen them in years. Slowly it all comes back to you as you remember with that quiet, sinking feeling: oh, that's right, you never shut up about your kids, do you? Even now that they are grown up. *'Brillo's a landscape gardener now. Ajax is a ski instructor and Vim has started her own business making eco-friendly pet clothes.'* Yes, it's all coming back to me now. Everything's bloody marvellous in your world, isn't it? Or it will be another trait that looms into focus as they witter on.

Now I remember! Your constant humble-bragging. That's exactly what used to get on my nerves about you. Listen to yourself. Still at it. 'Sorry I've got oil all over my hands. Damn car. Word of advice: never renovate a 1957 Jaguar XK140. Absolute nightmare. I'll be lucky if it's ready for the Goodwood Festival of Speed at this rate. What am I like?' Well, I won't answer that.

A surprise needs to be a happy fluke where need meets chance: you're really short on cash when you discover that a vinyl record that you've had for years happens to be worth a small fortune in some circles. Thank you, God. Thank you, Berlin Hitler Youth Choir. Here is the universe smiling upon you with an unexpected boon. Generally speaking, however, surprises are not welcome or enjoyable when they arrive in the form of a party. And the reasons for this are many, some of which are evident in this letter.

For many people, the fun of a party is in its anticipation. In this particular case, it's not unreasonable to assume that many of your girlfriends will have talked about it and even thought about what to wear. Nearer the time they might go shopping for an outfit, arrange to get their hair done and visit a nail bar. Without being able to do that as well, all you will have, in the shape of your fiftieth, is an evening with people who look miles better than you. I am therefore not in the least bit surprised that you are filled with trepidation. After all, the only truly excusable surprise party is a wake – and even then one usually has at least a week's notice.

However, you have written to me for advice and advice is what I will give.

Let's start by taking stock, as I think you will find that you

After all, the only truly excusable surprise party is a wake – and even then one usually has at least a week's notice

are actually holding a winning hand. You have a huge advantage in knowing that this surprise is afoot and that nobody knows that you know. That chance piece of information from the phone call has given you ample time to quietly prepare yourself physically and mentally for what could be a terrific and memorable night for you. Just imagine your joy, being 'surprised' by everyone you know while coincidentally looking your very best. Knowing you will be ready, therefore, will take the dread out of the plans that your adoring husband is making for you. After all, you almost certainly enjoy parties that you know are going to happen. If not, then we have to really interrogate Mark's motive for arranging something that he can accurately predict you will hate. That would be like sending a box of Snickers bars to an acquaintance you know has a serious peanut allergy. Or buying tickets to see an am-dram production of *Les Misérables* for someone who . . . well, for anyone.

To recap, then, you don't let on that you know about your surprise birthday party but, instead, you prepare yourself so that you are in the best possible frame of mind to have a great time. That said, we have to also consider the possibility that your terror of the upcoming event will prove too great an obstacle to overcome. Then what? It's clearly not acceptable to spend the next few months dreading the date and becoming more and more anxious. You'll resort to comfort eating and binge drinking until, come the big night, you look like a Cabbage Patch doll with a hangover. All your natural resilience will be worn down and you'll go along with Mark's pretence that you're going for a quiet night out, knowing full well what is in store for you. A hushed and darkened room above your local, bedecked with banners and balloons and filled with all your giggling friends waiting for the lights to come on so that they can all scream 'Surprise!' at you. If you do fear that you will be unable to cope with the stress, then, as I see it, you have two realistic options.

The first of these is to subvert the party. Contact everybody that Mark will have invited, as well as the landlord and the caterer. Let them know that Mark has been suffering delusional episodes and that his doctor has said that if he shows signs of manic planning, for example, then he will need to become an inpatient asap. If anyone hears from him and he sounds conspiratorial or secretive in any way, you would be grateful if they could quietly let you know. Then casually add that most of the time he is well and that you both spent the morning at the travel agent paying for a cruise that you are going on for your fiftieth and that you're hopeful the sea air will do him some good. I think that will flush everyone out and you can expect a batch of worried phone calls from invitees, many of whom – and I would bet my house on this – will confide that they thought Mark had sounded a bit strange when he contacted them. That is called the power of suggestion and it will work in your favour.

Alternatively, be up front, tell him what has happened and that you know about the surprise party. You can say that you appreciate the gesture but now that it's not a surprise, you would prefer to cancel and use the money to go on holiday, or whatever you like. If Mark is a reasonable man, he'll see sense in this, let everyone know and change the plans accordingly. If he's not such a reasonable man, he'll take it badly, sulk for a few weeks and tell everyone that you nosed around and found out about it, so what's the point? If he's a thoroughly unreasonable and maladjusted man he'll buy a baseball bat, arrange a surprise party to which only the caterer is invited and take things from there. The last of these is my least favourite and I am certainly not endorsing any form of retribution. I am simply pointing out a likely scenario. You might think that you know Mark well enough to be able to say he would never do that. I'm just saying that knowing someone and knowing what they are capable of in an emotional crisis are two different things. Until a couple of weeks ago you thought he would never do something as crass as arrange for all your friends and relatives to humiliate you in your favourite pub, didn't you? Food for thought, Kelly, food for thought.

So, there you have it. I very much hope that you are able to find a way to act the innocent but at the same time play this situation to your advantage. If not, you have other paths to follow which I hope will lead you out of this dilemma. Good luck, Kelly – and happy birthday.

Hi Jack, I basically have much less money than most of my friends and family yet am expected to buy my round when we all go out. How can I explain to them that this is unfair without coming across as tight-fisted?

(Via SMS)

I'm glad you've come to me about this as it is a complex issue which requires a professional solution. Before you meet up, give yourself a black eye and roll around in some dirt, then when you arrive, claim you were mugged on the way to the pub and had your wallet stolen. You will find that everyone buys you a drink without any expectation of you having to get a round in.

NB, this only works once. The third time I tried it friends were definitely starting to sniff a rat. Cheers.

Dear Jack, I am a man of 31 and am going bald after an accident when I fell out of a tree while on an outward-bound training course. Which hat should I wear so as not to cause offence? Thanks.

Lee, Enfield

Hello Lee. Try to think of your hair loss as a new beginning – like moving home, a career change or the birth of a child. Funnily enough, going bald is a lot like the birth of a child; it's tougher on women than it is on men and you spend the rest of your life wishing things could go back to how they were before. The fact that your concern is more pointed towards fashion than alopecia strongly suggests that you are simply a man not wanting to make a social gaffe.

Any hat is offensive in the wrong situation. It's really not that complicated. For instance it might be considered acceptable, on a hot day at the beach or a sports event, to wear one of those baseball caps fitted with beer cans strapped to each side and drinking straws that syphon the lager straight to your mouth. However, be prepared for the odd look of incomprehension if you wear the same hat to a funeral.

If you are still worried about the offence you could cause, maybe consider a hair-replacement procedure. It need only take a few hours of your time, usually looks quite good and nobody need ever know. Utmost discretion is a major consideration and most good clinics can guarantee this. That's why my neighbour Robin Jacobs at number 7, Rawling Avenue went to the Harley Street Hair Loss Centre. I must say, they did a pretty good job, although when I see him from my upstairs window his head does look a bit like mustard and cress grown by a child on wet toilet paper.

For some people a wig is a reasonable option and that's fair enough in my book. People lose their hair for all kinds of reasons, not all of them funny like yours, and remedying it with what is essentially a hat that looks like hair is a perfectly respectable solution. Especially when worn straight. But I would counsel against the toupee. No matter how well crocheted, a toupee has the unique ability to look comical in any setting. It's something about the way it just lies on top of your head, as lifeless as roadkill. The way it draws the onlooker's eye upwards and then immediately prompts an awkward, averting, sideways glance in a hopeless attempt at feigning obliviousness. The way a toupee can never really look natural and attractive, can never really blend into its environment like a fly-tipped mattress in a country lane. To all intents and purposes the toupee might just as well be a hat and, in answer to your question, the very hat not to wear if you don't want to offend.

Dear Jack, I've recently developed an irrational fear of anyth end in 'ing' (even typ this has been pretty traumatis!). Do you have someth that might help me with this debilitat condition?

Mark (via Twitter)

When I first reached out to the British public, offering a helping hand and the benefit of my wisdom, little was I to know how complex and disturbing some people's problems would be. First of all, Mark, a warning: I will be using words ending in ing. I have already done it three times and I won't be holding back. Sorry, but trying to avoid it throughout this piece runs the danger of reducing an otherwise serious response to the status of a tiresome parlour game – you know, the kind that friends play at get-to-gethers because they've realised they aren't really friends at all and need the distraction of an infuriating rule such as not being allowed to say 'Yes' or 'No' just to make the evening resemble a fun social event and not the life-sapping three hours of staring into the abyss of quiet despair that it really is.

You should be consoled by the fact that you are self-aware enough to recognise that you have a problem and want to do something about it. Many never reach that point and so live their entire lives in a state of delusion. It is on this point that the parlour game analogy is again useful. I have often noted that the most repressed people tend to be the ones who, given half the chance, will blithely instigate the most atrocious entertainments at a party. We've all been there and had to make up a hasty excuse and leave: 'Hey, listen up, everyone!' says Kenneth, the recently divorced project manager, 'I know a really great game. It's called pass the banana! What you do is you stand in a circle and pass a banana to the person next to you, but you can't touch it with your hands and it always has to go to a different part of the body. So, for instance, you hold it in your mouth and put it in between your neighbour's thighs and so on. Come on, it's a real laugh.'

At this point you already feel physically sick and are unsure if it's because of the M&S mini quiches washed down with room-temperature Prosecco or the prospect of being forced into this unpleasant ritual of borderline sex abuse masquerading as fun. If you're like me, you decide that it is most definitely the latter and that you are not going to indulge Kenneth's inappropriate request to, basically, sniff around everyone's private parts and get away with it scot-free. (My golden rule on occasions such as this is: never ever get involved in any party game that could conceivably end up with witness statements and things being put in evidence bags by a sickened-looking police officer.) At least you, Mark, recognise your shortcomings, unlike our friend Kenneth.

Having cleared that up, I will now turn my attention to your phobia. The fear of words, or logophobia, as smart-arses call it, is not uncommon. There is

> **The fear of words, or logophobia, as smart-arses call it, is not uncommon**

even an officially recognised fear of long words, which has, somewhat sadistically, been termed Hippopotomonstrosesquip-pedaliophobia. There are no known sufferers, but this is thought to be because those afflicted just can't bring themselves to say it. Tragic.

I wish I could say that your very specific anxiety relating to words ending with 'ing' is a well-researched disorder that receives generous funding from the World Health Organization, Pfizer, AstraZeneca, Comic Relief and the National Lottery. I wish I could tell you that doctors are excited by recent developments and that an announcement is imminent that will prove life-changing in the 'ingphobic' community. Alas, none of this is the case. The true picture is far less positive. To date, your problem has attracted zero interest among medics, counsellors, scientists or, indeed, the general public, including me. A recent survey even showed that 87 per cent of my readers actually skipped this bit because they just couldn't give a toss about your problem.

So my advice to you is to reach out on social media for fellow sufferers, form a support group where you can sit around drinking tea, eating too many custard creams and moaning about things. A lot of people seem to find that helpful and you might be one of them. Good luck.

> *Is having to give your name, address and telephone number to buy a takeaway coffee one step away from dictatorship or should we just be grateful we can still import coffee?*
>
> Fred (via Twitter)

Well, Fred, I am old enough to remember when takeaway coffee wasn't the ritualistic daily must-have that it is now. It's hard to believe that there was a time, within living memory, when people didn't consume a bucket of vaguely coffee-flavoured scorched milk every single morning of their working life. Nobody sat on the train constantly sipping and supping at their plastic nippled tub like a bored toddler with a beaker. We behaved like grown-ups back then: able to manage a moderate train or bus journey with little more than two or three cigarettes and an occasional tipple from the trusty hip flask. For an unexpectedly short period of my earlier life, I commuted as a student. An hour-and-a-half journey out to Staines. In fact, one of these days I will tell the full story of how I was, in my view, unjustly dismissed from my Airline Transport Pilot Licence course. It was only the second week of instruction and the steps up to the Boeing 747 flight simulator were, on that morning, again – in my humble opinion – hazardous enough to cause me to stumble. Twice. All right, three times if you include missing the bottom step due to inadequate lighting.

‘ **British Airways’ loss was the West London Rehab Clinic’s gain, so to speak** ’

But I still maintain that I was not, as later stated in the incident report, slurring my words when speaking with air traffic control. My explanation that the microphone in my comms set had developed a fault was rejected; however, I stand by it to this day.

Anyway, all water under the bridge. British Airways’ loss was the West London Rehab Clinic’s gain, so to speak. By the way, the coffee at the clinic was a feeble imitation because the inmates all had such addictive personalities that even caffeine represented a threat to their recovery, according to the staff, who never did work out how the centre got through so much hand sanitiser. (Surprisingly not that bad mixed with Fanta from the vending machine.) Dark times.

But I digress . . . rereading your question I can’t ignore a base note of paranoia in your language. A straightforward transaction has triggered a troubling fantasy in your mind. Your regular coffee stop has become a frightening place in which friendly baristas appear to you as strutting martinets, barking instructions and insisting on seeing ID before they can make your caramelaccino or chocoveganino or soyasaddo or whatever your choice is. For some reason you have interpreted a friendly request that you give your name – so that your drink can be delivered more efficiently – as an act of authoritarian aggression and you are now harbouring fears of national political upheaval that will result in a dictatorship.

It’s the kind of hallucinatory thinking that causes vagrants to start fights with invisible assailants and passing cars or, in my case, me at King's Cross railway station, Easter bank holiday, 2014. It's not an irrelevant example. Here was someone (it transpired that his name was Reece McConnor) who read my kindly intended act of dropping a 50p coin into his meekly clasped paper cup as an act of such aggression on my behalf that the only appropriate countermeasure was to attack me. Presumably British Transport Police keep copies of victim statements and, if so, it will be on record somewhere in the archives of King's Cross 'nick' that I had innocently not noticed that the cup being held by Reece McConnor was from Starbucks and, in fact, contained tomato soup – which, according to his statement, he was very much enjoying and which was ruined by my unsolicited donation. In the interests of fairness, I should also point out that McConnor was not, as I had assumed, a vagrant but a corporal in the Welsh Guards who was waiting to meet his wife and young child off the 12.47 from Doncaster. As I was to discover, he was still pretty stressed about his time serving in Kandahar a few years previously. As I see it, this doesn't exonerate him or excuse his violence towards me but does go some way to explaining his lightning-quick and, frankly, terrifyingly disproportionate reaction to a perceived threat.

You live and learn, as they say. According to the specialist I should eventually regain full use of my arm. As he said to me at my follow-up appointment, 'Luckily he knew what he was doing and it was a clean break.' I agree with the last part but nobody who saw Reece McConnor at the time of the assault could possibly have agreed that his demeanour was anything other than trancelike.

You finish your question with: '. . . or should we just be grateful we can still import coffee?' This is further evidence of the chaotic, rambling nature of your thought processes. In a single sentence you have ranted, expressed indignation, invoked elements of the Data Protection Act 2018, launched at least two conspiracy theories, warned of an imminent fascist coup and questioned our nation's trading status. I hope that it is not immodest of me to suggest you read my response to your question, not only for its obvious wisdom but as an example of clear, relevant, concise and logical reasoning.

I would like you to begin with some simple mental exercises that will relax you. Next time you go to order a coffee in a take-away outlet and the nice person serving you asks for your name, take a breath, slowly count to 5,* tell yourself, 'This is a nice thing. This is a friendly thing. She wants to know my name so that I get served the right coffee. I feel valued in this space. By giving my name I too am being friendly and I am cooperating. I do not need to be fearful in this situation. I am in a safe place.'

And then simply say to the assistant: 'Fred.' She will then write your name on the cup and you will get the coffee that you asked for: no confusion, no awkward mix-ups involving some pushy office worker taking your unnamed cup and you having to point out his mistake and him getting arsey with you and the whole thing escalating into an unfortunate incident with the two of you squaring up to each other and onlookers telling you to watch your language as there are children in there.

---

* Obviously don't count out loud or she will think you are either a basket case or that you actually call yourself 1-2-3-4-5 and write that on your cup, which considering your state of mind could result in you having a total meltdown and starting to yell at her that you are not a number, causing the police to be called who drag you out onto the pavement and sit on your face until you quieten down.

> Jack, I am 21 and am just coming to the end of my degree, the last year of which has been done mostly online due to Covid-19. I was enjoying university and really looking forward to my final year. To add to my annoyance, I made the decision not to take a gap year to travel like some of my mates did and I feel that I have probably lost out on a chance that I now might never have due to restrictions etc. When I leave uni I will have to find work of some sort which means that my travel options are limited by that as well. With limited time and finances I am trying to arrange a 3 month trip and was wondering what your advice would be regarding this generally, as well as where to travel to or where not to bother with. Much appreciated.
>
> Seb, Oxford

Thanks for writing to me, Seb. I predict that you are not alone – far from it. It's hardly a competition but I personally think that, apart from the elderly, your age group have probably had the toughest time of it.

I know that other age groups will feel overlooked reading this and therefore I will deviate for a moment to acknowledge some of them as well. So, big shout-out for parents of small children who found themselves incarcerated with their crawling-up-the-wall little darlings during the first lockdown, or 'holiday' as

> **The Victorians had it right when they told their kids that chimneys were fun things that were made for climbing up with a big brush between your teeth**

teachers called it. It's incredible to think how that particular bracket of mums and dads coped, especially when you consider that some of them won't have even had an exercise bike or running machine at home to strap their children onto for a few hours a day just to burn up a small fraction of their manic activity. I expect some child welfare groups will complain about my saying that so they definitely won't like this next bit either.

If my kids had been toddlers during that period, by the time it was over I would have patented some way of connecting them to the national grid and harnessing their energy for profit. There is nothing wrong in making a few quid out of them. The Victorians had it right when they told their kids that chimneys were fun things that were made for climbing up with a big brush between your teeth: 'First one back gets a glass of ale and half a pipe's worth of tobacco.' Everyone's a winner.

As for trying to teach social distancing to that age group, forget it. They're absolutely useless at it. Basically, we're talking about people who hold hands in the dinner queue just because they're standing next to each other. There is no point trying to explain social distancing to someone who thinks that biting your leg is a way of showing affection.

Nor should we forget the disappointment felt by older children who were unable to sit the exams that they'd been working towards. Personally, if that had happened to me at the age of sixteen or eighteen it would have made absolutely no difference. Most of my papers were returned 'ungraded', meaning that my results remain a mystery to this day.

From what I can see, today's teenagers are a diligent and tough-spirited lot who cracked on with their changed circumstances in a way that they can be proud of. Although, since we are being so honest with each other, I'll admit that I can't help but think there are a few young examinees out there who enjoyed their predictions rather more than they would have their results. There's nothing wrong with that. They deserve whatever bonuses they can get. But it probably should be noted that within this decade we will have a year group of doctors, accountants and engineers who, technically at least, don't have a GCSE between them. Just saying.

So I have some sympathy for your generation, Seb. Just as you see the gates of freedom opening before you, they slam shut in your face. Life should be a non-stop party at your stage in life. Obviously there are some who bail out sooner than others but they're easy enough to spot at an early stage. Ideally you should have identified them in your first year; they're usually the ones who arrive on day one with a padlocked biscuit jar and pre-written labels for the rest of their food. Why be that person? The one who puts a sticker on an opened can of pilchards so that nobody else takes it. On one level it makes perfect sense – the level that is otherwise referred to as 'loss of dignity'. The level that makes you the butt of humorous texts and nicknames for the rest of your life.

Anyway, back to the current situation. Before you move on to make your mark on the world, you wish to travel and compensate for the gap year that you didn't have when you left sixth form. It is only natural that you feel you have missed out in this respect. There is that old adage that says 'you can't miss what you've never had' but try saying that to someone who's browsing the internet; it is impossible to lead a modern life without constantly negotiating your way through a virtual gallery of things you've never had but somehow manage to miss very much. I realise that I have made it sound as though this is a kind of conditioning that is mysteriously imposed on us by some ethereal entity, but I haven't yet found a way to expand upon the subject without sounding like David Icke. For now, and because it is more relevant, I suggest we look at how your opinions about and attitude to travel have been formed by social media.

Not long ago, certainly within living memory, an invitation to look at somebody's holiday snaps was a running joke – something to be declined at any cost, especially if it involved a slide projector. The terror of being trapped in your neighbours' darkened front room as they delivered a two-hour TED Talk on their most recent trip to the Continent had become a suburban cliché by the mid-seventies. Luckily, the notion of a slide show eventually became so widely ridiculed that events of that nature became rarer and rarer until all the projectors were quietly consigned to a dusty loft and never spoken of again, except as a subject of mirth. In a sane universe, knowledge of how wretchedly dull pictures of other people's holidays really are would have passed into our genetic memory but, sadly, this is not a sane universe and no such evolution took place.

Only a few years later we were all at it again with our smart-phones. This time able to reach far wider audiences around the globe, twenty-four hours a day showing off where we were and what we had for breakfast. Whereas in the days of the slide projector, cackling jokes and smirks ultimately proved to be a good repellent, our neighbours today are far further afield, cannot hear our laughter and so persist with their posts without any concept of how unwanted they really are. This might not matter but the fact is that these unending image assaults are harmful to all of us, resulting in a general feeling of unease and dissatisfaction with one's own lot.

In part, I believe this is what has happened to you, Seb. Your exposure to social media has spiked a sense of envy and failure. Putting aside the narcissists on social media who treat us every day to selfies showing off their biceps, boobs, brunch, outfits, cars, kids, puppies, parties – the list is endless – we have a par-ticularly tiresome subset. This comprises travellers who never stop showing off about where they are, and how chilled it is there. It's hard enough to look at when you're my age and no longer have ambitions to travel because you've come to the conclusion that nowhere is so nice that it makes you forget the hassle of getting there or the prospect of having to repeat it all to get home again, but for you, it's almost unbearable. A feeling of envy is entirely understandable, but you will immediately be more content if you introduce a thread of scepticism to your thinking.

When somebody tweets a picture of themselves next to a waterfall in Phuket or in the back of a rusty charabanc sur-rounded by 'really cool locals' with caged chickens on their laps in Nepal, all you are actually looking at is a sunburnt show-off whose real dream destination, for all his travelling, is to be smirking on your phone. I call it 'travel-pouting'. That pose they strike for the camera when they're being snapped with the Sydney Opera House, a Moroccan goatherd or a snake-charmer in the background. The pose usually involves a cool hand gesture like a V-sign, not entirely unlike the one I do back at them.

Travel broadens your horizons, as the saying goes, but the saying never elaborates and states where you should travel to for this to happen. So it makes sense that a trip to Swindon (on your doorstep, practically) would have the same net effect as a trip to, say, Cambodia. It's still travel and, for what it's worth, I've been to Swindon loads of times and found it to be quite the eye-opener. Although do avoid Ken's Kebabs on Hinton Street unless you're OK with needing to suddenly stop on the drive home for some emergency crop spraying. There! You see? That's an experience that broadened my mind (stop it) and allowed me a small nugget of regional knowledge that I've been able to pass on to you. Was it done in the style of a bragging travel-pouter? No. Did I feel the need to tweet a selfie of me squatting in the lay-by with tears of pain running down my face? Absolutely not. I'm just telling you how it was without any of the know-it-all tips that travellers share with you, regardless of whether or not you asked them to: 'The food in Chiang Mai is totally amazing. Just don't eat the salad and you'll be fine.' You won't catch me sounding off with contradictory rubbish like that: 'The food at Ken's Kebabs is amazing. Just don't eat the kebabs and you'll be fine.' Even though that is actually true.

Obviously I'm not really telling you never to travel long distance as there are clearly advantages, especially for your parents who get to rent your room out. So in the event that you do finally decide that touring Swindon is less exhilarating than going round the world – and I'm not here to judge you either way – then you might like to give some thought to the following suggestions that will help you not come back bleating on like a hostel-hopping bore. In simple terms, then, please try to avoid the following when you return. And I aim this advice not just at you, Seb, but at all travellers who I might meet at some point in the future.

- Don't tell me that I must go to a particular place 'before it changes'. It incenses me to have to first of all listen to a monotonous description of some godforsaken town or country and then to be told I have to go there preferably by the end of the month to see it before the inevitable creep of modernism 'spoils' it all. *'It's just so incredible, right, the little place where we stayed was literally so basic, it was made of corrugated iron and they had like earth on the floor and you had to get your water from a puddle and boil it on an open stove, like right in the street. You really should go before it all changes. I mean already they've got a massive doctor's surgery being built, which is pretty sad actually.'* To me, that sounds like somewhere that I would prefer to visit when it *has* all changed. There's no hurry. I can wait until they get basic infrastructure and, preferably, a Marriott as well, thanks anyway.
- *'The people there are so friendly.'* This is particularly mad-

dening as it shows such naivety. Unless you unknowingly wandered into Disneyland, there is nowhere that you can accurately say this about. For the most part, people are friendly to tourists because they see them as great big $ signs waddling about, haemorrhaging money at every street-food stall they pass. I can offer no better proof of this than the fact that research shows that most tourists visiting London find the people there friendly. London. Even more pitiful is when you encounter one of those grief junkies who makes it their business to explore war-torn countries and finds everyone to be really hospitable and warm. Really? The people there are traumatised, scared and desperate – do you honestly believe that they're smiling at you for any reason other than hoping you haven't come to steal their livestock and set fire to their village? Next time, maybe stay away and watch *Panorama* instead. I've yet to watch a documentary about a civil war and make the mistake of thinking that the people in it look friendly and are probably waving their machetes and AK-47s as some quaint form of greeting.

- '*Of course, it is best if you avoid all the touristy bits.*' Is it? Why? I *am* a tourist and so are you for that matter. Touristy bits are there for a reason. They're there so that you know where the locals want you to go and where they'd rather you stayed away from. And who can blame them for that? It's an unspoken request by them for a bit of privacy but one which you, in your insatiable quest for novelty, decided to ignore. Not content with seeing the ancient temple, visiting the hair-braiding district, watching the traditional dance display and touring the spice markets in a rickshaw pulled by a nine-year-old, you had to go and stick your sweaty nose in where it's not wanted and poke around their homes as well, didn't you? They're not washing their clothes in the river or grinding corn with a fence post to give you a terrific photo opportunity – that's what the dancing was for, you prick.

- '*The takeaway you get here is good but nothing like the real thing that you get over there.*' Look, it's noodles and ribs. I know it's not as good as the '*little place you used to go to in Da Nang*' but it's passable, and besides, the moped guy doesn't go that far.

- '*I remember once when I was right up near the border I went into a hut that was actually a restaurant and they had a wooden board with a rat and a parrot and a gecko nailed to it and that was the menu.*' Good for you. Personally, I prefer those laminated menus in a leatherette cover that you can read while you eat your prawn crackers. '*Yeah, actually they don't really have prawn crackers in—*' Oh, shut up.

- '*I went to Ko Phangan to find myself.*' Mmmm! Weird how nobody goes to Weston-super-Mare or Whitley to find themselves, isn't it? Why can't people like that just say they went on holiday instead of making out it was a religious retreat? Just admit it, you're a bum and you went to Thailand to laze around on a beach with all the other bums who go there. The proof is that you came back none the wiser. It's not like you returned with a new and enriched worldview and a set of spiritual principles by which to live your life. You didn't. You returned with a load of duty-free and a dose of crabs. Then they tell you that what's really great about it is that you can live on 70p a day, including beer and as much rice as you can eat. Well, three cheers for the Third World. Next time try Lidl; it's closer.

- *'I got this incredible carpet from a woman in a market in this town in northern India. It actually took her mother and three daughters nearly a month to make. Paid the equivalent of £25 for it. She wanted 35 but you have to haggle, otherwise they don't respect you.'* These ones leave me speechless – poverty fetishists who'll now spend their lives bragging they have witnessed true deprivation but failing to mention or even realise how they managed to make it just that little bit worse.

Another part of your question concerns only having three months available for your travels but don't worry, that should give you plenty of opportunity to do the things that you want to. While it is the case that most people your age take a year for this, it's also true that they are usually only fully conscious for about a quarter of it, meaning that if you manage to remain fairly sober you will be quids in with all your mates. I know there are some people who return from their travels claiming to have found authenticity in far-distant lands but that usually only means that they got injured on a zip wire and had to be medivacked home and it's the most exciting thing that's ever happened to them; or they met this really cool Ozzie backpacker who went native, became a Buddhist and is now running a flip-flop repair kiosk in Pa Tong; or a friend of a friend of theirs was blackmailed into being a drug mule and got caught at the airport with three condoms of heroin in his colon and is now in a Bangkok prison eating cockroaches, fagging for the jail daddy and writing to the British embassy for help at least four times a day. Almost always their adventures are vicarious, exaggerated or plain untrue. Undoubtedly one of the great advances of the late twentieth century is that travel was made available to the masses. The not so great part is that the masses all came back with highly unlikely stories that we've had to listen to ever since.

This is not a call for greeting every tale of adventure with a raised eyebrow and deflating scepticism, just a reminder to keep the salt cellar close at hand. Season to taste and enjoy the meal, that's the trick. Did Flo really see polar bears from inside her tent? Yes, because the tent was overlooking Toronto Zoo, but so what? She enjoyed it. Did Emma and Joel actually hitch lifts on lorries across Australia? If you allow that the lorries had wings and Qantas written on the side, I suppose so, yes. In the scheme of things, what does it matter? What's the point of an open ticket if you don't use it? Was Alex arrested and threatened with imprisonment for political agitation in Thailand or did he in fact just get a hard smack round the head from a policeman for wandering into a temple in his beach gear, sipping a can of lager? Who knows? I only know what I hope happened.

By using your time wisely, Seb, you too can come back filled with memories that, although not believed by all, will sustain you through life's duller periods. Even if the

> **Did Flo really see polar bears from inside her tent? Yes, because the tent was overlooking Toronto Zoo**

grand tour does not deliver the rich source of anecdotes you had expected, make up your own and stand by them. It is partly your adventures that will inspire the next year group to travel, after all. Good luck, Seb.

Acknowledgements

My sincere thanks to Jane Sturrock, Charlotte Fry, Milly Reid, Lipfon Tang, Bruno Vincent and Séan Costello at Quercus for their help and support. Also to Joe Norris, Amy Dillon, Alison Peters and everyone at Off The Kerb.

Index